"The world was peopled
with wonders."

The origin of Wildsam comes from above, a
line of prose in the novel, *East of Eden,* written by
John Steinbeck. Six words hinting at a broad and
interwoven idea. One of curiosity, connection, joy. And
the belief that stories have the power to unearth the
mysteries of a place — for anyone. The book in
your hands is rooted in such things.

Special thanks to the University of Southern California
Cinematic Arts Library, the Hugh M. Hefner Moving Image
Archive, the Los Angeles Public Library, Santa Monica
Mountains National Recreation Area, Jenny Eccles and the
USC Libraries, Glen Creason, Christina Rice, Lynell George,
Josh Kun, Phillip Washington, Los Angeles County Metro
Transit Authority, Ben Fuqua, Brian and Jessie DeLowe,
Hannah Henderson, Raan and Lindsay Parton, Cindy Kirven,
Stan and Judy Coleman, Luke Lombardo, Besha Rodell, David
Parker and Zach Behrens.

WILDSAM FIELD GUIDES™

Copyright © 2018

Published in the United States
by Wildsam Field Guides, Austin, Texas.

ISBN 978-1-4951-5539-0

Art direction by SDCO Partners
Illustrations by Caroline Tomlinson

To find more field guides, please visit
www.wildsam.com

⇛ CONTENTS ⇚

⟫ WELCOME ⟪

WHENEVER I GO TO LOS ANGELES, there's a feeling that follows me around, a low hum just above my subconscious. It's a pale nostalgia with an itch of déjà vu. Driving on Sunset or Mulholland. Looking up at every skyduster palm or down the Malibu pier. In L.A., the hazy air of familiarity is tough to shake.

If you grew up with a television, you sort of grew up in Los Angeles. Take the Quality Café. This nothing-special diner sits on 7th Street, just west of downtown. It shares a block with a mini-mart, a skate shop, a shoe repair, a liquor store, an indie rock venue and a psychic — a Bukowskian row near-perfect as ode to the city. Today, the big red letters once painted above the façade are gone. The OPEN sign ten years flipped around. But inside, the squeaky booths and Formica tables and countertop griddles remain. As do faint traces of *Mad Men*'s Don Draper. Denzel in *Training Day*. *Old School* and *Catch Me If You Can*. Morgan Freeman sipping the thin coffee, two separate times, in *Se7en* and in *Million Dollar Baby*.

In 1909, when early filmmakers were trekking out from Chicago, advertising their "plays without words" and framing up studios in what was then called Edendale, they spoke of Los Angeles in almost mystical terms. They talked about the magical sunlight. "We have tried every part of the world," one producer told the *Los Angeles Times* that same year. "This is the best place."

What I've found to be true, more than Hollywood's faded reflection, is that the off-camera Los Angeles, the undone city with countless neighborhoods, tangled-up foodways, heady doses of broken spots and troubles — all lit up by that same eternal sun — that *that* L.A. is far more compelling than any TV version. Culver City and Compton. Silver Lake and El Segundo. Pacific Palisades and Pasadena. Everywhere spinning and waning and dying and shimmering back to life again. *-TB*

ESSENTIALS

FOODWAY

French Dip
In a food fight of historic proportions, old-school establishments Philippe's and Cole's have been battling over the rights to this prized local creation—roast beef piled high on a French roll with a side of au jus—since 1908.

RECORD COLLECTION

Pet Sounds	The Beach Boys
Mellow Gold	Beck
The Runaways	The Runaways
Déjà Vu	Crosby, Stills, Nash & Young
Blood Sugar Sex Magik	Red Hot Chili Peppers
Straight Outta Compton	N.W.A
Beauty and the Beat	The Go-Go's
Jackson Browne	Jackson Browne
How Will the Wolf Survive?	Los Lobos
Good Kid, M.A.A.D City	Kendrick Lamar
The Doors	The Doors
Fear Fun	Father John Misty
Blue	Joni Mitchell

ESSENTIALS

PROGRESS

- Smog conditions improving, from 234 high-ozone days in 1978 to 81 in 2015
- Weekly ridership on Metro subway and light rail hits 9.6 million, up 2 million since 2010
- In 2016, film production activity increased to 39,605 shoot days
- Ranked #3 US city for open access to municipal data, up from #17 in 2014
- Silicon Beach startups received nearly $3 billion in funding in 2016, six times more than in 2012
- Though up slightly since 2014, homicides are drastically lower than in 2016 [294] than 1992 [1,094]
- In Elysian Valley, federal officials approved $1.3 billion plan to revitalize 11 miles of river habitat

CHALLENGES

- The 2013 *Los Angeles Health Atlas* revealed that a South L.A. resident will live five years less than one living in other parts of the city
- Since 2010, L.A. has added 179,000 new residents, but fewer than 25,000 new housing units
- According to an LAUSD report, 840 weapons were collected in schools during 2014-15 academic year
- Angelenos spend 45% more time in traffic, making it the second-most congested city in North America, after Mexico City
- In metro area, 58% of renters pay more than 30 percent of their income toward rent
- From Oct 2016 to Feb 2017, downtown L.A. received more than 13 inches of rain, 216% more than average

STATISTICS

35	Nobel Prizes won by Caltech faculty and alumni
54	Percentage of residents speaking language other than English at home
284	Sunny days per year, on average
8%	Likelihood of 8.0 earthquake before 2050
10,064 feet	Mt. Baldy, highest point in L.A.
136%	Growth of "gig employment" in 2014, third-highest spike in US

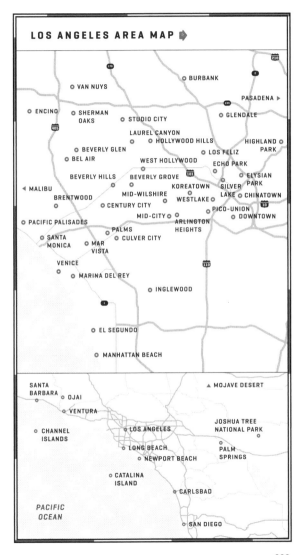

LOS ANGELES AREA MAP ➡

BESTS

*A curated list of Angeleno favorites, including
strip-mall sushi, doughnut shops, hidden bars, drive-in movies,
flea markets, comedy clubs, fancy spas and more*

» FOOD & DRINK «

For more distinctive L.A. dishes, see our
CLASSICS map on page 57.

NEIGHBORHOOD SPOT
Little Dom's
2128 *Hillhurst Ave*
littledoms.com
Trust the corner joint for Old Fashioneds and Grandma's spaghetti.

....

SUSHI
Soregashi
6775 *Santa Monica*
soregashi-la.com
Strip-mall gem specializing in chirashi bowls and izakaya-style small plates.

....

DINER
Millie's Cafe
3524 *W Sunset Blvd*
milliescafela.com
Morning winner for "messes and scrambles" and nine different Benedicts.

CHOPPED SALAD
La Scala
434 *N Canon Dr*
lascalabeverlyhills.com
Lettuce, salami, garbanzo beans, mozzarella and Leon's secret dressing.

TACOS
Tire Shop Taqueria
4069 *S Avalon Blvd*
Nothing-special digs house this Tijuana-style carne asada destination. Nights only.

....

NEW INSTITUTION
Gjelina
1429 *Abbot Kinney*
gjelina.com
Travis Lett's sceney spot anchors the new Venice, doubly so with sibling bakery, Gjusta.

DOUGHNUTS
Randy's Donuts
805 *W Manchester Blvd*
randysdonuts.com
Unquestionable icon of 1950s L.A., sublime sugar bombs and a rooftop tribute.

....

FOOD HALL
Grand Central Market
317 *S Broadway*
grandcentralmarket.com
Dozens of delicious options for hungry wanderers in a reborn landmark.

....

PIZZA
Mozza
641 *N Highland Ave*
pizzeriamozza.com
The secret is Nancy Silverton's pastry-chef-obsessive dough recipe.

CAFETERIA

Clifton's
648 S Broadway
cliftonsla.com
Part hot line, part
cabinet of curiosity,
with a tiki lounge
upstairs. Ya dig?

....

KOREAN BBQ

Park's BBQ
955 S Vermont Ave
parksbbq.com
New favorites—
snappy pork belly
and hyper-fermented
kimchi—plus what
many consider the
best traditional Ko-
rean food in town.

....

TOAST

Sqirl
720 N Virgil Ave
sqirlla.com
Cultish cuts of
brioche, ricotta
and jam or JJ's
avocados and pick-
led carrots.

....

VEGAN MEXICAN

Gracias Madre
8905 Melrose Ave
graciasmadreweho.com
Plant-based versions
of Mexican favor-
ites like chilaquiles
and enchiladas.

KAISEKI

n/naka
3455 Overland Ave
n-naka.com
A modern spin on
traditional Japa-
nese tasting menus.
Thirteen courses,
$185 a person.

....

HIDDEN BAR

The Walker Inn
3612 W 6th St
thewalkerinnla.com
Behind a secret door
at The Normandie
Club, a speakeasy
where reservations
are clutch.

....

ITALIAN

Bestia
2121 E 7th Pl
bestiala.com
The husband-
and-wife-owned
DTLA spot
marries from-
scratch pastas with
industrial vibes.

....

CREOLE

Harold & Belle's
2920 W Jefferson Blvd
A Leimert Park
staple serving
Louisiana classics
since 1969. Order
the bayou catfish.

FRENCH

Petit Trois
718 Highland Ave
petittrois.com
Chef Ludo's 22-seat
love note to the
idyllic Paris bistro.

....

STEAKHOUSE

Musso & Frank Grill
6667 Hollywood Blvd
mussoandfrank.com
Claims the finest dry
martini and most dap-
per red blazers in L.A.

....

WINE LIST

A.O.C.
8700 W 3rd St
aocwinebar.com
France and Califor-
nia, by the glass, and a
Beard-winning menu.

....

WORKING LUNCH

Polo Lounge
9641 Sunset Blvd
Choose a garden table
at the Beverly Hills
Hotel. Oysters, Cae-
sar, Wagyu burger.

....

TIKI

Tiki-Ti
4427 W Sunset Blvd
tiki-ti.com
The math: 12 stools,
94 tropical drinks
and 1 Ray's Mistake.

»» SHOPPING «««

*For more fashion outposts, see our
STYLE map on page 69.*

SPIRITS
Bar Keeper
*3910 W Sunset Blvd
barkeepersilverlake.com*
Vintage bar tools, hard-to-find bottles and the finest bitters collection in L.A.

....

DISTRICT
Abbot Kinney Blvd
Venice
Mile-long stretch includes Stag, Tortoise, Stahl + Band, Chariots on Fire, Urbanic, Bazar and dozens more.

....

BOOKSTORE
Skylight
*1818 N Vermont Ave
skylightbooks.com*
Thriving indie with quirky clubs and big-name author visits.

SUCCULENTS
California Nursery Specialties
19420 Saticoy St
Find a wealth of native desert beauties at the "Cactus Ranch."

....

FURNITURE
Sunbeam Vintage
*106 S Avenue 58
sunbeamvintage.com*
Midcentury finds from Dorothy Thorpe glassware to bygone bar carts.

....

SKATEBOARDS
L.A. Skate Co.
*5401 Santa Monica
laskate.com*
Rife with L.A. skate history and a crazy selection of boards and roller skates.

VINTAGE CARS
Back in the Day
21126 S Avalon Blvd
In the market for a 1956 baby-blue Bel Air? Head to this showroom off the 405.

....

MOTORCYCLES
Deus Ex Machina
*1001 Venice Blvd
deuscustoms.com*
Temple to all things dude, chiefly the badass custom bikes built in-house.

....

DESIGNER CLOTHES
Ron Herman
*8100 Melrose Ave
ronherman.com*
Longtime tastemaker stockist with good mix of runway and indie brands.

SODAS

Galco's Old World Grocery

5701 York Blvd
galcos.com

Fizzmaster John Nese carries 500 varieties. Try the Bubble Up.

....

GUITARS

McCabe's

3101 Pico Blvd
mccabes.com

Moonlights as a world-class venue: Joni Mitchell and Jackson Browne both played here.

....

HOME

County Ltd.

1837 Hyperion Ave
countyltd.com

Opened in 2016, it's perhaps the perfect L.A. shop: part Eames acolyte, part Tokyo tastemaker.

....

VINTAGE EYEWEAR

Hotel de Ville Vintage Eyewear

7422 Beverly Blvd
hoteldevilleeyewear.com

Deadstock frames, new styles from Europe and a house line of sunnies.

LIFESTYLE

Apolis & Alchemy Works

826 E 3rd St
apolisglobal.com
alchemyworks.us

One lines the closet; the other fills living room and beyond.

....

SURF GEAR

Zuma Jay's

22775 Pacific Coast Hwy
zumajays.com

Opened by a former Malibu mayor, it's a must for boards and gossip.

....

BOHEMIAN

General Store

1801 Lincoln Blvd
shop-generalstore.com

Jesse Kamm clothing, small-batch scents and home goods with a Joshua Tree feel.

....

MODERN GIFT

Midland

8634 Washington Blvd
Culver City
shop-midland.com

Southwestern vibes in this new purveyor of indie finds.

T-SHIRTS

Filth Mart

1038 N Fairfax Ave
filthmart.net

Thinnest, softest, rarest of vintages, like a tattered $200 Mötley Crüe tee.

....

PAPER GOODS

Poketo

8840 Washington Blvd
poketo.com

Modern stationery and minimalist planners keep correspondence and calendars up-to-date.

....

WEEKEND VENDORS

Melrose Trading Post

7850 Melrose Ave
melrosetradingpost.org

Every Sunday at Fairfax High School, 200 sellers plus next-level people-watching.

....

TYPEWRITERS

Rees Electronics

2140 Westwood Blvd
startypewriters.com

Click, clack and ding at this depot for vintage Olivettis and Underwoods.

⫸ ACTION ⫷

For more excursions, see our
ADVENTURE map on page 56.

VISTA

Stahl House
1635 *Woods Dr*
stahlhouse.com
Arrange a private
tour of this
Laurel Canyon
modernist study.

....

DRIVE-IN

Electric Dusk
2930 *Fletcher Dr*
electricduskdrivein.com
L.A.'s only open-
air cinema. No car?
No problem. Cozy
up on AstroTurf
seating.

....

CLASSICAL MUSIC

Hollywood Bowl
2301 *Highland Ave*
hollywoodbowl.com
Gustavo Dudamel
leads the L.A. Phil-
harmonic's summer
concert series.

SKATEPARK

Venice Skatepark
1800 *Ocean Front Walk*
veniceskatepark.com
Watch boarders
swoop and grind
across smooth
concrete pits.

....

ODDITY

Museum of Jurassic Technology
9341 *Venice Blvd*
mjt.org
Dimly lit ode to
natural phenomena,
anthropology, and
dreamlike genius.

....

GARDEN

Descanso Gardens
1418 *Descanso Dr*
descansogardens.org
Over 150 acres of
oak forest, specimen
roses, 60 types of
cycads and more.

HORSE RACING

Santa Anita Park
285 *W Huntington Dr*
santaanita.com
Made famous by
Seabiscuit lore, holds
prominent derby for
3-year-olds each April.

....

OUTDOOR FLEA

Rose Bowl
1001 *Rose Bowl Dr*
rgcshows.com
2,500 dealers on sec-
ond Sundays. Come
around sunrise to
snag vintage Levi's.

....

PRIVATE COLLECTION

Getty Center
1200 *N Sepulveda Blvd*
getty.edu
Arts citadel includes
masterworks, but
it's Robert Irwin's
Central Garden that
stands out.

STARGAZING

Griffith Observatory
2800 E Observatory Rd
griffithobservatory.org
Public astronomy
center, perched on
Mount Hollywood.
Free since 1935.

....

LIVE MUSIC

The Troubadour
9081 Santa
Monica Blvd
troubadour.com
Rolling Stone ranked
it America's #2 small
venue. The 400-seat
space boasts a six-
decade history of
American music.

....

DAY SAILING

Bluewater Sailing
13505 Bali Way
bluewatersailing.com
Fleet of small boats
and friendly skip-
pers for half days
out to Catalina or
up to Malibu.

....

BACK ROAD

Angeles Crest
Highway
A scenic, curvy
path over the
San Gabriel Moun-
tains. Turn up the
Jackson Browne.

LINE DANCING

Cowboy Country
Saloon
3321 E South St
cowboycountry.mu
Beloved outlier
features three
dance floors, a
poolroom, a
restaurant, two
bars and one me-
chanical bull.

....

SILENT MOVIES

Cinefamily
611 N Fairfax Ave
cinefamily.org
On Second Satur-
days, the "Silent
Treatment" series
plays rare flicks from
the pre-sound era.

....

ARCHITECTURE

Architecture
Tours L.A.
architecturetoursla.com
The "city of the
future" via Pasadena,
Hollywood, Hancock
Park, or a special
Frank Gehry tour.

....

OPEN MIC

The Comedy Store
8433 W Sunset Blvd
thecomedystore.com
The easiest place
to bomb in town,

thanks to frequent
"Show Up Go Up"
open mic nights.

....

CONTEMPORARY ART

The Broad
221 S Grand Ave
thebroad.org
This honeycomb
cube was one of the
most hyped open-
ings of 2016. FYI,
it's "brode."

....

JUKEBOX

The Drawing Room
1800 Hillhurst Ave
Opens at 6 a.m.
sharp and rocks
the finest CD
slinger in town.

....

WELLNESS

The Springs
608 Mateo St
thespringsla.com
Calling this
a spa is like
calling a Ferrari
a car; it's 13,500
square feet of
healing arts.

....

SUP YOGA

YOGAqua
yogaqua.com
Paddle out for
90-minute sessions
in Marina del Rey.

»» EXPERTISE ««

Cameron Weiss
weisswatchcompany.com
From his 2,100-foot
Torrance studio,
Weiss goes beyond
handsome time-
pieces.
....

Thom Mayne
morphosis.com
The Pritzker Prize-
winning provoca-
teur's work includes
the inside-out com-
plex at Emerson
College on Sunset.
....

Dr. Melina Abdullah
calstatela.edu
Scholar-activist
and department
chair focuses on
race, gender and
oppression.

Megan Ellison
annapurna.pictures
Her quick rise
to prominence
[and serious indus-
try cred] sparked
by *Zero Dark
Thirty* and *Ameri-
can Hustle*.
....

Steve Clarkson
*steveclarksondream
maker.com*
His academies have
tutored more than
200 college QBs.
....

Miles MacGregor
elmac.net
The L.A. native's
landmark murals
imbue everyday
Angelenos with a
spiritual glow.

Garrett Leight
garrettleight.com
Launched Venice
optical brand-shop
in 2011, blending
timeless style with
easygoing Califor-
nia vibes.
....

Kelly Wearstler
kellywearstler.com
Playful glamour seen
in hotels—Viceroy
and Proper chains—
and her luxury
atelier on Melrose.
....

Hillary Justin
blissandmischief.com
Vintage pro
specializing in
denim rarities
for collectors and
fashion A-listers.

HATMAKER
Nick Fouquet
nickfouquet.com
A dozen pre-made styles are available, or you can commission a custom topper.

....

MIXOLOGIST
Justin Pike
thetastingkitchen.com
Try his King of the Dudes cocktail made from rye, Punt e Mes and tree bark syrup called *mamajuana*.

....

BARBER
Todd "Sween" Lahman
sweeneytoddsbarbershopla.com
Lahman's 1947 barbershop remains Chandler-era specific, right down to the 1950s magazines.

....

GALLERIST
Lisa Overduin
overduinandco.com
Propelled L.A.-made art—such as Guy de Cointet pieces that were languishing in garages and attics—to the fore.

YOGA
Maty Ezraty
matyezraty.com
Co-founded original Yoga Works in Santa Monica; beloved teacher to dozens of Angeleno yogis.

....

CURATOR
Michael Govan
lacma.org
Avant-garde flair for theatrics enlivens LACMA in the form of performance art and public spectacles.

....

NIGHTLIFE
Cedd Moses
213hospitality.com
From the Golden Gopher to Broadway Bar, his nine-bar empire helped revitalize downtown.

....

RIVERKEEPER
Lewis MacAdams
folar.org
This poet and activist is working to secure a $1.3 million grant to re-naturalize parts of the L.A. River.

JUICEMASTER
Amanda Chantal Bacon
moonjuiceshop.com
Mother Nature and Earth Mother rolled into one, Bacon started a movement with her plant alchemy.

....

SURFBOARD SHAPER
Bill Stewart
stewartsurfboards.com
"Father of the modern longboard" and airbrusher for SoCal brands like Ocean Pacific.

....

PODCASTER
Marc Maron
wtfpod.com
His *WTF* podcast series has enough mojo to lure Barack Obama to the garage studio.

....

RACE AND POLITICS
Eso Won Bookstore
esowonbookstore.com
Since 1990, the Leimert Park spot has been a global go-to for literature about the African-American experience.

ALMANAC

*A deep dive into the cultural archives of
Los Angeles through timelines, newspaper clippings, letters,
lists, taxonomies and other historical hearsay*

LOS ANGELES V. SAN FRANCISCO

*In July of 1923, California's two of-record newspapers sent reporters to
write a week's worth of columns aimed at "stating frankly what he thinks
of the other man's town." Below are excerpts from Harry Carr, the* Los
Angeles Times' *contributor to the good-natured rivalry.*

July 8, 1923

I love San Francisco. Los Angeles is all right in a way, but it is too noisy
and too busy. It gets on my nerves. The streets are filled with people
rushing around making money and finding oil wells and adding new real
estate tracts to the landscape. You can't get into any of the hotels because
the tourists walk all over you. You can't find your way around because Los
Angeles is growing new streets faster than the postmaster can keep track
of them.

July 9, 1923

To me, San Francisco is a Russian wolf hound. Fastidious, aristocratic,
aloof. Beautiful with the beauty of romance and imagination.... Los
Angeles is a white bull terrier. His hide is a little soiled and his voice is a
little raucous. He dives in among the automobile wheels, upsets all the
garbage cans on both sides of the street, gets into a few friendly fights by
way of entertainment, and is all wrong most of the time. But oh, how he
does love life! He just loves everybody.

July 11, 1923

When you come to examine the essence of its soul you find that Los
Angeles is a women's town. San Francisco is a man's town....There
may have been a time when pioneering was a man's job. But I don't
really believe it. Men go into new countries, snoop around, shoot a few
wild animals, dig up some gold, have a few fights and wander on. No
pioneering country ever amounts to anything until the women arrive.
Then it begins to get settled and to progress.

IN-N-OUT BURGER

A locals guide to 15 off-menu orders at L.A.'s fast food institution

4X4
Four beef patties and four slices of cheese.

3X3
See 4x4, sub 3's for 4's.

GRILLED CHEESE
Your typical burger, sans beef.

THE FLYING DUTCHMAN
A grilled cheese with beef patties subbing for bread. [Extra tip: Add fries to the middle.]

ANIMAL-STYLE
Arm-slicking upgrade adds mustard-grilled patty, pickles, extra "spread" and grilled onions.

ANIMAL-STYLE FRIES
Smothered in cheese, grilled onions, special sauce.

MONKEY-STYLE
Standard burger topped with Animal-style fries.

ROADKILL FRIES
Animal-style fries with a Flying Dutchman on top.

NEAPOLITAN SHAKE
Exactly what it sounds like: strawberry, chocolate and vanilla ice cream, all in shake form.

FRIES, TO ORDER
Want your fries crispy? Just order them "well done."

PROTEIN-STYLE
Standard burger with the buns swapped out for lettuce.

MUSTARD-GRILLED PATTY
For maximum flavor, mustard is grilled into patty before anything hits the bun.

LEMON-UP
Genius blend of lemonade [regular or pink] and 7-Up.

WHOLE GRILLED ONION
Instead of chopped, ask for whole slices grilled up for your burger.

DOGGY-STYLE
The ultimate off-menu combo: one Protein-Style Grilled Cheese with fries inside the sandwich.

PALM TREES OF NOTE

*Now emblematic of Los Angeles, palm trees of all but one variety
[California Fan Palm] are actually non-native to L.A., planted with
especially robust efforts in the 1930s to promote the area's exotic,
magical appeal — the city as one big movie set.*

PLANT	DESCRIPTION
California Fan	*Petticoat skirt of dead fronds forms cozy habitat for small birds*
King	*Stately native to Australia with deep green fronds*
Travellers	*Banana-like leaf stems hold rainwater in case of emergency*
Queen	*Graceful elders along Highland Ave, between Melrose and Wilshire, given monument status*
Canary Island	*Resembles a pineapple in its infancy, famous feathery tops as adults*
Mexican Fan	*Skinny-trunk skydusters can top 90 feet, very camera friendly*
Pygmy Date	*Smallish subtropical fruit-bearing ornament to gardens*
Pindo	*One of the hardiest varieties, withstanding the rare freeze*
Triangle	*Madagascar origins, triad frond pattern is a head turner*
Bismarck	*Noble specimens with silvery leaf crowns up to 10 feet wide*
Fishtail	*Native to Asia, unusual leaves resemble jagged fishtails*
Windmill	*Resort-style looks, often planted near swimming pools*
Royal	*Ashen white trunk, "Palm Sunday" leaves up to 10 feet long*
Ponytail	*Swollen trunk base stores water, not a true palm*

"PARADISE"

American Mercury
March 1933

In this prescient but oft-overlooked essay, prominent mystery novelist
James M. Cain [The Postman Always Rings Twice, Mildred Pierce]
pays tribute to the real-life virtues of early 20th-century L.A.

Wash out the palm trees, half visible beyond the tap dancing platform. Palm trees are here, but they are all phonies, planted by people bemused with the notion of a sub-tropical climate, and they are so out of harmony with their surroundings that they hardly arrest your notice. Wash out the movie palazzos, so impressive in the photographs. They are here too, at any rate in a place called Beverly Hills, not far from Hollywood; but they are like the palm trees, so implausible in their surroundings that they take on the lifelessness of movie sets. Above all, wash out the cool green that seems to be the main feature of all illustrations got out by railroads. Wash that out and keep it out.

When you have got this far, you can begin quite starkly with desert. As to what this desert looked like before it was touched by man you can get an idea by following it across the Mexican border into Lower California, where man is feeble and touches no more than he has to. On one side you can put an ocean, a placid oily-looking ocean that laps the sand with no sign of life on it except an occasional seal squirming through the swells, and almost no color. On the other side, some hundreds of miles inland, put some mountains. Between ocean and mountains, put some high hills that look as if they were spilled out carelessly with a gigantic sugar scoop, and between the hills, wide, flat valleys. Have both hills and valleys a gray, sunbaked tan; put a few tufts of dry grass on the hills and occasional clumps of stunted trees in the valleys, but see that the naked earth shows through everything that grows on it.

You are now ready for the handiwork of man. I suggest that you put it in with water-color, for if it blurs here and there, and lacks a very clear outline, that will be so much the better. The hills you can leave just as they were. In the valleys, in addition to the stunted clumps you already have, put in some trees: a few palms, eucalyptus, orange, fig, pomegranate, and other varieties that require little water. You might smear in some patches of green lawn, with hose sprinkling them: it will remind you that bringing water in by pipeline is still the outstanding accomplishment of man in this region.

KDAY 93.5

In the early 1980s, a scrappy L.A. station called KDAY 1580 AM flipped the script on mainstream radio by devoting its airtime almost exclusively to hip-hop. Led by legendary program director Greg Mack, KDAY launched the careers of some of the genre's biggest stars, including a young Compton DJ named Dr. Dre. Today, the station continues to celebrate the good old days of rap over at 93.5 FM.

"Nuthin' But a 'G' Thang"	Dr. Dre
"Dear Momma"	2Pac
"Next Episode"	Dr. Dre
"It Was a Good Day"	Ice Cube
"Poison"	BBD
"California Love"	2Pac
"Hip Hop Hooray"	Naughty by Nature
"Wild Thing"	Tone Lōc
"Juicy"	The Notorious B.I.G.
"Keep Ya Head Up"	2Pac
"Push It"	Salt-n-Pepa
"You Can Do It"	Ice Cube
"Going Back to Cali"	The Notorious B.I.G.
"To Live and Die in LA"	2Pac
"Atomic Dogg"	George Clinton
"Big Pimpin'"	Jay Z
"Double Dutch Bus"	Frankie Smith
"Ain't No Fun"	Snoop Dogg
"Bust A Move"	Young MC
"Ain't No Future"	MC Breed
"Ms. Jackson"	OutKast
"Hypnotize"	The Notorious B.I.G.
"I Ain't Mad at Ya"	2Pac
"I'm Not Your Puppet"	Hi-C
"Gin and Juice"	Snoop Dogg

NORMAN MAILER

Esquire, November 1960

It is not that Los Angeles is altogether hideous, it is even by degrees pleasant, but for an Easterner there is never any salt in the wind; it is like Mexican cooking without chile, or Chinese egg rolls missing their mustard; as one travels through the endless repetitions of that city which is the capital of suburbia with its milky pinks, its washed-out oranges, its tainted lime-yellows of pastel on one pretty little architectural monstrosity after another, the colors not intense enough, the styles never pure, and never sufficiently impure to collide on the eye, one conceives the people who live here—they have come out to express themselves, Los Angeles is the home of self-expression, but the artists are middle-class and middling-minded; no passions will calcify here for years in the gloom to be revealed a decade later as the tessellations of hard and fertile work, no, it is all open, promiscuous, borrowed, half bought, a city without iron, eschewing wood, a kingdom of stucco, the playground for mass men—one has the feeling it was built by television sets giving orders to men.

TIKI DRINKS

Along with Don the Beachcomber and Trader Vic's, The Luau in Beverly Hills, open from 1953 to 1978, pushed Polynesian cocktails into the mainstream. Below, a sample of Luau offerings from a 1953 menu:

Tahitian...A bit of Tahiti, Isle of Passion and Romance, made of the nectar of passion fruit...$1

Bo-Lo...Hawaiian pineapple filled with liquid sunshine and the fragrance of the Jasmine... $1.75

Luau Grog...Eight separate ingredients go into this one. Neither weak nor lusty...$1.50

Dr. Fong...Alias Dr. Funk. Mysterious yet delightful...$.90

Steve's Pearl...For ladies only. Should be delicately sipped—not gulped...$1

MAGIC

In a city of megawatt stars, the toughest ticket in the 1980s was for NBA games when Magic Johnson captained the "Showtime" Lakers

Mar 1979	Epic rivalry with Larry Bird begins in NCAAs
Jun 1979	Drafted first overall by Los Angeles Lakers
May 1980	Wins NBA championship, replacing Kareem Abdul-Jabbar [knee] in deciding game and scoring 42 points
Nov 1980	Hurts left knee, misses 45 games during season
Jun 1981	Signs 25-year, $25 million contract, the richest in sports history at the time
Nov 1981	Magic "not having any fun" in boring offense; Laker owner fires coach Paul Westhead, replaces with Pat Riley
Jun 1982	"Showtime" fast-tempo style leads to championship
May 1984	Loses to Larry Bird's Celtics, famously no air-conditioning in Boston Garden for Game 7
Jun 1985	Magic beats Bird, averaging 14 assists a game in Finals
May 1988	Wins fifth NBA title over Detroit Pistons
Jun 1991	Falls to Michael Jordan and Chicago Bulls
Nov 1991	At Forum Club, Magic announces that he is HIV positive; "I plan to go on living for a long time," he says
Aug 1992	Leads Olympic "Dream Team" in Barcelona Games
Sep 1992	Un-retires from Lakers, though rumbling and worry among other players causes Magic to leave NBA in November
Apr 1994	Launches nationwide chain of movie theaters
Feb 1998	Partners with CEO Howard Schultz to open 100 Starbucks in underserved urban neighborhoods
Mar 2012	Joins group to buy the Dodgers for $2 billion
Apr 2012	Broadway play *Magic/Bird* debuts in New York City
Jan 2016	Magic's net worth estimated at $500 million
Feb 2017	Returns to Lakers as President of Basketball Operations; tells *USA Today*, "I want to call the shots"

ROCKET MAN

In 1984, William "Bill" Suitor made history by piloting an aeronautics "rocket belt" into the Los Angeles Olympics Opening Ceremony. More than a decade later, he was still flight-testing the latest designs.

April 14, 1995

Dear Mr. Barker,

Thank you for my appointment as Chief of Flight Test Operations for your new 1995 Rocket Belt. No one has successfully completed such a device since the Tyler belt, which is now over 20 years old! When I came to Houston to inspect your Rocket Belt, I was overwhelmed at the quality and improvements you and your staff have made in this new Rocket Belt. I can honestly say that you have created "the finest Rocket Belt ever built."

I am very excited to be a part of "Keeping the Dream Alive." In 1964, I was hired by Bell Aerosystems at the behest of Wendell Moore [the original inventor of the Rocket Belt] to fly his invention of 1961. Subsequently I have worked with and piloted every known Rocket Belt ever built.

Wendell Moore was my neighbor as I grew up over 30 years ago; unfortunately, he died in May of 1969. I shall be forever grateful to him for the opportunities he brought to my life. At the moment his "Dream" is on hold. In 1988, I wrote in my manuscript that "neither the right amount of interest, nor the right amount of money exists for the full realization to be achieved, but maybe someone, somewhere, will have the right amount of his or her own 'Right Stuff' to get it off the ground again." I am delighted to have found the people with the interest and ability to "Keep the Dream Alive." I hope to start a Wendell F. Moore Memorial Science Scholarship Fund at our local high school in Youngstown, New York, to help some student that has the aptitude as well as the attitude to get the education needed to continue Wendell's dream.

I fully endorse your Rocket Belt [which I have named "Pretty Bird"] as a Marvelous Jewel, unequalled to any previous creation of its type, anywhere.

In closing, I'd like to say that I am truly honored to be a part of your team.

Sincerely,

William P. Suitor

CHINATOWN

Below, a pivotal scene from Robert Towne's famous Chinatown *screenplay [widely regarded as Hollywood's "perfect script"].*

EXT. MULWRAY HOME - DUSK

By the pond, cigarette smoke drifts INTO SHOT. A car pulls up. In a moment Cross can be SEEN, looking TOWARD CAMERA.

> **CROSS**
> There you are.

He walks toward Gittes who stands by the pond, smoking.

> **CROSS**
> [CONTINUING]
> Well, you don't look any the worse for wear, Mr. Gittes, I must say... where's the girl?...

> **GITTES**
> I've got her.

> **CROSS**
> Is she all right?

> **GITTES**
> She's fine.

> **CROSS**
> Where is she?

> **GITTES**
> With her mother.

Cross' tone alters here.

> **CROSS**
> ... with her mother?

Gittes pulls something out of his pocket and unfolds it.

> **GITTES**
> I'd like you to look at something, Mr. Cross —

> **CROSS**
> [TAKING IT]
> What is it?

> **GITTES**
> An obituary column... can you read in this light?

> **CROSS**
> Yes... I think I can manage...

Cross dips into his coat pocket and pulls out a pair of rimless glasses. He puts them on, reads. Gittes stares at the bifocal lenses as Cross continues to look through the obituary column. He looks up.

> **CROSS**
> What does this mean?

> **GITTES**
> — that you killed Hollis Mulwray —

Gittes is holding the bifocals with the broken lens now.

> **GITTES**
> [CONTINUING]
> — right here, in this pond. You drowned him... and you left these.

Cross looks at the glasses.

> **GITTES**
> ...the coroner's report showed Mulwray had salt water in his lungs.

> **CROSS**
> [FINALLY]
> Hollie was always fond of

tide-pools. You know what
he used to say about them?

GITTES

Haven't the faintest idea.

CROSS

— that's where life
begins... marshes,
sloughs, tide-pools...
he was fascinated by
them... you know when
we first came out here
he figured that if you
dumped water onto desert
sand it would percolate
down into the bedrock
and stay there, instead
of evaporating the way
it does in most reservoirs.
You'd lose only twenty
percent instead of
seventy or eighty. He
made this city.

GITTES

— and that's what you were
going to do in the Valley?

EXT. POND - CROSS AND GITTES

CROSS

[AFTER A LONG MOMENT]

— no, Mr. Gittes. That's
what I am doing with the
Valley. The bond issue
passes Tuesday — there'll
be ten million to build an
aqueduct and reservoir. I'm
doing it.

GITTES

There's going to be some

irate citizens when they
find out they're paying for
water they're not getting.

CROSS

That's all taken care of.
You see, Mr. Gittes. Either
you bring the water to L.A.
— or you bring L.A. to
the water.

GITTES

How do you do that?

CROSS

— just incorporate the
Valley into the city so the
water goes to L.A. after all.
It's very simple.

Gittes nods.

GITTES

[THEN]

How much are you worth?

CROSS

[SHRUGS, THEN]

I have no idea. How much
do you want?

GITTES

I want to know what you're
worth - over ten million?

CROSS

Oh, my, yes.

GITTES

Then why are you doing it?
How much better can you
eat? What can you buy that
you can't already afford?

CROSS

[A LONG MOMENT, THEN:]

The future, Mr. Gittes,
the future. Now where's
the girl?...

"DEATH IN HOLLYWOOD"

Evelyn Waugh, 1947

Penned for Life *magazine, Evelyn Waugh's faux anthropological study [excerpted here] satirizes the opulent burial practices observed at Forest Lawn Memorial Park and other high-profile resting places.*

In a thousand years or so, when the first archaeologists from beyond the date line unload their boat on the sands of Southern California, they will find much the same scene as confronted the Franciscan missionaries. A dry landscape will extend from the ocean to the mountains. Bel Air and Beverly Hills will lie naked save for scrub and cactus, all their flimsy multitude of architectural styles turned long ago to dust, while the horned toad and the turkey buzzard leave their faint imprint on the dunes that will drift on Sunset Boulevard.

For Los Angeles, when its brief history comes to an end, will fall swiftly and silently. Too far dispersed for effective bombardment, too unimportant strategically for the use of expensive atomic devices, it will be destroyed by drought. Its water comes 250 miles from the Owens River. A handful of parachutists or partisans anywhere along that vital aqueduct can make the coastal strip uninhabitable. Bones will whiten along the Santa Fe Trail as the great recession struggles eastward. Nature will reassert herself and the seasons gently obliterate the vast, deserted suburb. Its history will pass from memory to legend until, centuries later, as we have supposed, the archaeologists prick their ears at the cryptic references in the texts of the 20th century to a cult which once flourished on this forgotten strand; of the idol Oscar, sexless image of infertility; of the great Star Goddesses who were once noisily worshiped there in a Holy Wood.

THE BRONCO CHASE

Partial transcript of LAPD detective Tom Lange's June 17, 1994, phone call with O.J. Simpson, recorded as Simpson departed his Brentwood house in a white Ford Bronco after his wife, Nicole Brown Simpson, was discovered murdered.

LANGE: O.J., it's Tom again.

SIMPSON: Ah—[moaning]

LANGE: Hey, it's going to be better tomorrow. Get rid of the gun. Toss it, please. Too many people love you, man. Don't give it all up. Don't hurt everybody. You're going to hurt everybody.

SIMPSON: I'm just going to leave. I'm just going to go with Nicole. That's all I'm going to do. That's all I'm trying to do.

LANGE: Hey, listen—think about everybody else.

SIMPSON: I just can't do it here on the freeway. I couldn't do it in the field. I went to do it at her grave. I want to do it at my house.

LANGE: You're not going to do anything. Too many people love you. Your kids, your mother, your friends, A.C., everybody. You've got the whole world. Don't throw it away.

SIMPSON: Ah—

LANGE: Don't throw it away, man. Come on. O.J.? Hello? Lost him again.

[Phone connection cuts off]

Two of 2016's most celebrated television shows focused on the complexities of the Simpson trial. First, FX's The People vs. O.J. Simpson: American Crime Story, *a ten-part scripted drama starring Cuba Gooding, Jr. as the accused, as well as John Travolta, Sarah Paulson, Courtney B. Vance, David Schwimmer and others. It won 9 Emmy Awards. Second, Ezra Edelman's ESPN documentary,* O.J.: Made in America, *a nearly 8-hour exploration of race, celebrity and the city of Los Angeles itself that was called "a masterwork of scholarship, journalism and cinematic arts" by Mary McNamara of the* Los Angeles Times. *Edelman's documentary won universal acclaim, as well as an Oscar.*

EAMES

Life Magazine, 1950

Charles Eames, whose stark, comfortable chairs in the last five years have made him the best-known U.S. designer of modern furniture and a winner in the Museum of Modern Art furniture competition, recently designed a house and adjoining studio for himself near Santa Monica, Calif. As might be expected of a man whose chief concerns are simplicity, functionalism and economy, Eames's own house is simply built of steel trusses, bright stucco panels and great curtained expanses of glass. It is extraordinarily functional, built for a couple that likes to live without servants or cocktail parties and work surrounded by the varied objects that interest them. And when work or contemplation pall, the Eameses have the ocean just across the meadow from their home.

Eames likes to say his job is "the simple one of getting the most of the best to the greatest number of people for the least." Few men are so earnestly dedicated to their jobs. To feed an insatiable interest in the looks of things, he and his wife take frequent sleeping-bag trips into the surrounding seaside and desert areas collecting weeds, rocks and driftwood whose appearance they want to study. They decorate their home with Chinese fans, Indian blankets and the golden eggs for the same reason. Eames has a distaste for the superfluous which sometimes even affects his speech: "Take chair by wall," he may invite a visitor. Commented awed movie director Billy [*Sunset Boulevard*] Wilder, "He even has the guts to sit there and be quiet if he hasn't anything to say."

---

*To watch Charles Eames speak at length about
his philosophy of chair design, search online for "Science in
Action: The Chair," a 1960 television program produced
by the California Academy of Sciences.*

LAUREL CANYON

*In the '60s and '70s, this woodsy Hollywood enclave drew
counterculture musicians who would weave folk and country
influences into rock 'n' roll, changing popular music forever.*

From "Our House" [1970]
Written by Graham Nash,
recorded by Crosby, Stills, Nash
& Young
*I'll light the fire, you place the
flowers in the vase that you
bought today*
*Staring at the fire for hours and
hours while I listen to you*
*Play your love songs all night long
for me, only for me*

....

From "Trouble Child" [1974]
Written and recorded by
Joni Mitchell
They open and close you
Then they talk like they know you
They don't know you
*They're friends and they're
foes too*
Trouble child
*Breaking like the waves
at Malibu*

....

From "Revolution
Blues" [1974]
Written and recorded by
Neil Young
*I got the revolution blues, I see
bloody fountains,*
And 10 million dune buggies

comin' down the mountains
*Well, I hear that Laurel Canyon
is full of famous stars,*
*But I hate them worse than lepers
and I'll kill them in their cars*

....

From "Twelve Thirty [Young
Girls Are Coming to the
Canyon]" [1967]
Written by John Phillips,
recorded by the Mamas &
the Papas
*Young girls are coming to the
canyon*
*And in the mornings I can see
them walkin'*
*I can no longer keep my blinds
drawn*
*And I can't keep myself from
talkin'*

....

From "Peaceful Easy Feeling"
[1972]
Written by Jack Tempchin,
recorded by the Eagles
*I like the way sparkling
earrings lay*
Against your skin so brown
*And I want to sleep with you
in the desert night*
With a million stars all around

DISNEY'S NINE OLD MEN

In the late 1920s and early '30s, a group of nine gifted animators joined Walt Disney's early creative team, helping to envision and animate the most beloved and memorable characters and scenes in Disney lore. The Nine Old Men created the 12 Basic Principles of Animation, such as "squash and stretch," anticipation drawing and the "slow in, slow out" rule.

ANIMATOR	LEGACY
Frank Thomas	*The Queen of Hearts, Cinderella's Wicked Stepmother, Bambi on ice*
Les Clark	*Early Mickey Mouse work, Snow White's Dwarfs, Dumbo*
Marc Davis	*Snow White, Tinker Bell, Cruella de Vil, animatronic ride design*
Ollie Johnston	*Cinderella's stepsisters, Ichabod Crane, Thumper from* Bambi
Milt Kahl	*The Fairy Godmother, Tigger, Mowgli and Baloo, Mary Poppins' hounds*
Ward Kimball	*Jiminy Cricket, the Mad Hatter, Tweedledee and Tweedledum*
Eric Larson	*The Lady and the Tramp, Br'er Rabbit, 3 Little Pigs, Prince Charming*
John Lounsbery	*Captain Hook, Merlin, Eeyore, Piglet,* Fantasia's *"Dance of the Hours"*
Wolfgang Reitherman	Peter Pan's *crocodile, the Headless Horseman,* Pinocchio *whale scene*

SPIRITUALITY

In the last 100 years, Los Angeles has drawn seekers and visionaries of all sorts, from new age to evangelical to apocalyptic. Below, five of the most famous leaders.

AIMEE SEMPLE MCPHERSON
International Church of the Four Square Gospel
Echo Park's Angelus Temple was this radio preacher and healer's megachurch from 1923 until 1926, when she disappeared during a swim. One month later, McPherson turned up in Mexico, claiming to be kidnapped, and was charged with fraud.

....

L. RON HUBBARD
The Church of Scientology
Hubbard wrote sci-fi in a North Hollywood trailer before introducing his religious doctrines to the world, including thetans, the E-meter, Dianetics and Sea Org's billion-year contracts. Its first Celebrity Centre was opened in Los Angeles in 1969.

....

CHARLES MANSON
The Manson Family
Before the murders, before the retreat into Death Valley, before his name became synonymous with every burned-out hippie-cult fear of the 1960s, Charlie Manson was an aspiring musician with some ultra-devoted groupies who communed in Topanga Canyon.

....

DAVID BERG
Children of God [aka The Family]
A Christian cult founded in L.A. in 1968, The Family lured new members through a practice they called "flirty fishing"—wherein female followers attracted lonely men with sexy promises—and apocalyptic rhetoric.

....

JIM "FATHER YOD" BAKER
The Source Family
Baker crafted his love cult on a blend of Western mystery traditions, yoga-ish Eastern philosophy and a trendy vegan restaurant on Sunset that Marlon Brando loved. Father Yod is rumored to have had 14 wives in his Hollywood Hills utopian mansion.

THE WATTS REBELLION

On the night of August 11, 1965, a 21-year-old black man named Marquette Frye, driving his mother's 1955 Buick, was pulled over by a white Highway Patrol officer, Lee W. Minikus. Minikus suspected drunk driving [a charge Frye later admitted was true]. But as the routine stop unfolded, crowds gathered and bristled, and the scene boiled over in a swarm. The disorder that night burst into a six-day riot in South-Central Los Angeles. "It was an all-out war zone," one sergeant remarked about the Watts neighborhood, which was a historically poor section of Los Angeles with substandard housing, failing schools and high unemployment. One *Los Angeles Times* editorial went so far as to call the riots "an orgy of lawlessness." On the other hand, Dr. Martin Luther King, Jr., said this, on August 20: "These were the rumblings of discontent from the 'have nots' within the midst of an affluent society.... It is my opinion that these riots grew out of the depths of despair which afflict a people who see no way out of their economic dilemma." In all, the havoc resulted in $40 million in property damage, 34 deaths and over 3,400 arrests. After extensive civic studies, very few of the recommended measures were instituted to improve life for African Americans in the Watts community. And less than 30 years later, the 1992 L.A. riots would eerily recall those heady days.

CASE STUDY HOUSES

In the 1940s and '50s, Arts & Architecture *commissioned 36 glassy, modernist abodes, many of which still glow in the Los Angeles hills.*

☞Case Study House #1
  10152 *Toluca Lake Ave*

....

☞Case Study House #8 [Eames]
  203 *Chautauqua Blvd*

....

☞Case Study House for 1953
  1811 *Bel Air Rd*

☞Case Study House #17
  9554 *Hidden Valley Rd*

....

☞Case Study House #21
  9038 *Wonderland Park Ave*

....

☞Case Study House #22 [Stahl]
  1635 *Woods Dr*

AMELIA EARHART

The Toluca Lake, California-based aviator set numerous records throughout her illustrious career, including six solo-flight first attempts. Below, a pilot's-eye view of those legendary trips in Earhart's own words.

....

A 1935 diary entry, following her 1935 successful solo flight from Honolulu to Oakland, the first ever:

> I had the cockpit window open a bit and the cold rain beat in on me until I became thoroughly chilled. I thought it would be rather pleasant to have a cup of hot chocolate. So I did, and it was. Indeed that was the most interesting cup of chocolate I have ever had, sitting up eight thousand feet over the middle of the Pacific, quite alone.

Her final diary entry, on her attempted 1937 circumnavigation of the globe, written on the island of New Guinea just before her mysterious disappearance over the Pacific:

> Not much more than a month ago I was on the other shore of the Pacific, looking westward. This evening, I looked eastward over the Pacific. In those fast-moving days which have intervened, the whole width of the world has passed behind us—except this broad ocean. I shall be glad when we have the hazards of its navigation behind us.

Undated letter to husband George Palmer Putnam, to be read if her flight should end in disaster:

> Please know I am quite aware of the hazards. I want to do it because I want to do it. Women must try to do things as men have tried. When they fail, their failure must be but a challenge to others.

HOLLYWOOD SIGN

By 1978 the Hollywood sign, erected in 1923 with four additional letters to advertise the Hollywoodland real estate development, was in ragged shape. Led by *Playboy* publisher Hugh Hefner and glam rocker Alice Cooper, nine sponsors—one for each letter—pledged $27,777.77 to restore it.

H	*Terrence Donnelly, newspaper publisher*
O	*Giovanni Mazza, film producer*
L	*Les Kelley,* Kelley Blue Book *publisher*
L	*Gene Autry, actor and country-western singer*
Y	*Hugh Hefner,* Playboy *publisher*
W	*Andy Williams, pop singer*
O	*Warner Bros. Records*
O	*Alice Cooper, glam-rock singer*
D	*Dennis Lidtke, nightclub owner*

HOW TO PRONOUNCE "LOS ANGELES"

In 1908, Charles Lummis, a former *Los Angeles Time*s editor and outspoken regional booster, launched a public campaign to stop English speakers from—as he saw it—butchering the pronunciation of Spanish place names, especially Los Angeles. He summarized his case in a brief rhyme, which publications across the nation printed with some amusement.

"Our Lady, The Queen of the Angels"

The Lady would remind you please,
Her name is not Los Angie Lees,
Nor Angie anything whatever.
She hopes her friends will be so clever
To spare her fit historic pride
The G shall not be jellified.
O long, G hard, and rhyme with "yes"
And all about Loce Ang—el—ess.

BOB HOPE AND RICHARD NIXON

April 17, 1974

Rose Mary Woods
Executive Assistant and
Personal Secretary
The White House
Washington, DC

Dear Rose Mary:

Thank you very much for that article by Tricia Nixon Cox. Who would ever have believed at the inaugural in 1973 that we would be looking at a statement like that. But that is politics.

In my traveling about the country, I have talked with many people but it seems the media only prints what they want and the other side is not giving up and going to try to stretch this whole Watergate mess into 1976. It's giving dirty politics a bad name, that all I know. Nobody knows better than you because you are close to it.

Its amazing every time the President made a personal appearance all you see is people smiling, people cheering. Where do these other people hide?

Anyway keep a stiff upper lip as we old English say. Give my best to the President and tell him to hit the golf course once in a while as difficult as that might be. It would be a great relaxer for him.

Dolores joins me in sending our warmest regards.

Signed
BOB

POBLADORES

In the summer of 1781, 44 *Mexican settlers trekked from Sonora and Sinaloa to establish the pueblo of Los Angeles. Like the Franciscan priests who founded missions and the soldiers who set up presidios, these towns-people, or* pobladores, *formed the vanguard of Spanish colonization in the Alta California territory. Thanks to official records that carefully noted each settler's racial caste, we know these people were an ethnically diverse bunch. Most claimed mixed ancestry [mulato/a or mestizo/a], more than half had African ancestry, and only two were full-blooded Spaniards.*

↳ Camero, Manuel [Mulato] and María Tomasa [Mulata]

....

↳ Lara, José Fernando [Español], María Antonia [India], and three children

....

↳ Mesa, Antonio [Negro], María Ana [Mulata], and two children

....

↳ Moreno, José [Mulato], and María Guadalupe [Mulata]

....

↳ Navarro, José Antonio [Mestizo], María Regina [Mulata], and three children

....

↳ Rodriguez, Pablo [Indio], María Rosalia, and one child

....

↳ Quintero, Luis [Negro], María Petra [Mulata], and five children

....

↳ Rosas, Basilio [Indio], María Manuela [Mulato], and six children

....

↳ Rosas, Alejandro [Indio] and Juana María [India]

....

↳ Vanegas, José [Indio], María Bonifacia [India], and one child

....

↳ Villavicencio, Antonio Clemente [Español], María Seferina [India], and one child

MOVIE DISASTERS

*Hollywood has a long and creative history of
destroying Los Angeles on the big screen.*

DESTRUCTIVE FORCE	FILM
Martian heat rays	*War of the Worlds*, 1953
60-foot man	*War of the Colossal Beast*, 1958
Biological plague	*The Omega Man*, 1971
Gelatinous monster	*The Blob*, 1972
Comet dust, zombies	*Night of the Comet*, 1984
Nukes	*Miracle Mile*, 1988
Earthquake, floods	*Escape from L.A.*, 1996
Alien mothership	*Independence Day*, 1996
Volcano lava bombs	*Volcano*, 1997
Tornadoes	*The Day After Tomorrow*, 2004
Careless superhero	*Hancock*, 2008
Mayan prophecy	*2012 The Movie*, 2009
Cyclone of sharks	*Sharknado*, 2013

GAME SHOWS

*Since the 1950s, the studio-heavy exurban hubs of Burbank, Century
City and Studio City—otherwise known as the "Center of the Game Show
Universe"—have been turning out some of the most memorable hits [and
misses] in entertainment history. Here are just a few of the gems produced
here over the years—both with and without a live studio audience.*

⇨ Jeopardy!
⇨ The Price Is Right
⇨ Time Machine
⇨ Wordplay
⇨ You Don't Say
⇨ Super Password
⇨ All-Star Secrets
⇨ Wheel of Fortune
⇨ What's This Song?
⇨ Battlestars

⇨ Card Sharks
⇨ Celebrity Sweepstakes
⇨ Let's Make a Deal
⇨ Classic Concentration
⇨ Hollywood Squares
⇨ Supermarket Sweep
⇨ It Could Be You
⇨ Truth or Consequences
⇨ The Weakest Link
⇨ Scrabble

THE PERFECT GAME

Broadcaster Vin Scully spent 67 years as the play-by-play man for the Dodgers, both in Brooklyn and in Los Angeles. Millions of fans know his Sinatra-smooth voice and crisp eye for detail. Scully's ninth-inning call of Sandy Koufax's 1965 "perfect game" is regarded as the masterpiece of live sports announcing. It is printed below in its entirety.

Three times in his sensational career has Sandy Koufax walked out to the mound to pitch a fateful ninth where he turned in a no-hitter. But tonight, September the 9th, nineteen hundred and 65, he made the toughest walk of his career, I'm sure, because through eight innings he has pitched a perfect game. He has struck out 11, he has retired 24 consecutive batters, and the first man he will look at is catcher Chris Krug, big right-hand hitter, flied to second, grounded to short. Dick Tracewski is now at second base and Koufax ready and delivers: curveball for a strike.

Oh and 1 the count to Chris Krug. Out on deck to pinch-hit is one of the men we mentioned earlier as a possible, Joey Amalfitano. Here's the strike 1 pitch to Krug: fastball, swung on and missed, strike 2. And you can almost taste the pressure now. Koufax lifted his cap, ran his fingers through his black hair, then pulled the cap back down, fussing at the bill. Krug must feel it too as he backs out, heaves a sigh, took off his helmet, put it back on and steps back up to the plate.

Tracewski is over to his right to fill up the middle, Kennedy is deep to guard the line. The strike 2 pitch on the way: fastball, outside, ball 1. Krug started to go after it and held up and Torborg held the ball high in the air trying to convince Vargo but Eddie said nossir. One and 2 the count to Chris Krug. It is 9:41 p.m. on September the 9th. The 1-2 pitch on the way: curveball, tapped foul off to the left of the plate.

The Dodgers defensively in this spine-tingling moment: Sandy Koufax and Jeff Torborg. The boys who will try and stop anything hit their way: Wes Parker, Dick Tracewski, Maury Wills and John Kennedy; the outfield of Lou Johnson, Willie Davis and Ron Fairly. And there's 29,000 people in the ballpark and a million butterflies. Twenty nine thousand, one hundred and thirty-nine paid.

Koufax into his windup and the 1-2 pitch: fastball, fouled back out of play. In the Dodger dugout Al Ferrara gets up and walks down near the runway, and it begins to get tough to be a teammate and sit in the dugout and have to watch. Sandy back of the rubber, now toes it. All the boys in the bullpen straining to get a better look as they look through the wire fence in left field. One and 2 the count to Chris Krug. Koufax, feet together, now to his windup and the 1-2 pitch: fastball outside, ball 2. [Crowd boos.]

A lot of people in the ballpark now are starting to see the pitches with their hearts. The pitch was outside, Torborg tried to pull it over the plate but Vargo, an experienced umpire, wouldn't go for it. Two and 2 the count to Chris Krug. Sandy reading signs, into his windup, 2-2 pitch: fastball, got him swingin'!

Sandy Koufax has struck out 12. He is two outs away from a perfect game.

Here is Joe Amalfitano to pinch-hit for Don Kessinger. Amalfitano is from Southern California, from San Pedro. He was an original bonus boy with the Giants. Joey's been around, and as we mentioned earlier,

he has helped to beat the Dodgers twice, and on deck is Harvey Kuenn. Kennedy is tight to the bag at third, the fastball, a strike. 0 and 1 with one out in the ninth inning, 1 to nothing, Dodgers. Sandy reading, into his windup and the strike 1 pitch: curveball, tapped foul, 0 and 2. And Amalfitano walks away and shakes himself a little bit, and swings the bat. And Koufax with a new ball, takes a hitch at his belt and walks behind the mound.

I would think that the mound at Dodger Stadium right now is the loneliest place in the world.

Sandy fussing, looks in to get his sign, 0 and 2 to Amalfitano. The strike 2 pitch to Joe: fastball, swung on and missed, strike 3! [Crowd cheers.]

He is one out away from the promised land, and Harvey Kuenn is comin' up.

So Harvey Kuenn is batting for Bob Hendley. The time on the scoreboard is 9:44. The date, September the 9th, 1965, and Koufax working on veteran Harvey Kuenn. Sandy into his windup and the pitch, a fastball for a strike! He has struck out, by the way, five consecutive batters, and that's gone unnoticed. Sandy ready and the strike 1 pitch: very high, and he lost his hat. He really forced that one. That's only the second time tonight where I have had the feeling that Sandy threw instead of pitched, trying to get that little extra, and that time he tried so hard his hat fell off—he took an extremely long stride to the plate—and Torborg had to go up to get it.

One and 1 to Harvey Kuenn. Now he's ready: fastball, high, ball 2. You can't blame a man for pushing just a little bit now. Sandy backs off, mops his forehead, runs his left index finger along his forehead, dries it off on his left pants leg. All the while Kuenn just waiting. Now Sandy looks in. Into his windup and the 2-1 pitch to Kuenn: swung on and missed, strike 2!

It is 9:46 p.m.

Two and 2 to Harvey Kuenn, one strike away. Sandy into his windup, here's the pitch:

Swung on and missed, a perfect game!

[38 seconds of cheering.]

On the scoreboard in right field it is 9:46 p.m. in the City of the Angels, Los Angeles, California. And a crowd of 29,139 just sitting in to see the only pitcher in baseball history to hurl four no-hit, no-run games. He has done it four straight years, and now he caps it: On his fourth no-hitter he made it a perfect game. And Sandy Koufax, whose name will always remind you of strikeouts, did it with a flurry. He struck out the last six consecutive batters. So when he wrote his name in capital letters in the record books, that "K" stands out even more than the O-U-F-A-X.

FERNANDOMANIA

Mexican-born pitcher Fernando Valenzuela made his Dodger debut on opening day 1981. Quickly, the lefty's in-game verve [and nasty screwball] sparked what became known as "Fernandomania" in L.A. and throughout the big leagues. His starts drew sellout crowds and fans went wild for his matador-like windup and command. After becoming the only player to win both the Cy Young and Rookie of the Year awards in one season, that October Fernando helped lead the Dodgers to a World Series victory over the New York Yankees.

PÍO DE JESÚS PICO

During the 19th century, L.A. survived the death of one empire [the Spanish] and conquest by another [the US], all the while growing from a tiny agricultural village into a budding metropolis. As the last governor of Mexican Alta California [the territory north of Baja that became the state of California], Pico had a front-row seat.

1805	Born a Spanish subject at Mission San Gabriel Archangel, Alta California.
1821	Becomes a Mexican citizen following independence from Spain.
1826	Wins seat in territorial *diputación*, or legislature.
1828	Receives first land grant from Mexican government for 8,922 acres near San Diego.
1832	Leads successful revolt against unpopular governor Manuel Victoria; briefly becomes governor of Alta California himself.
1834	Supports the secularization of California's missions; paves the way for mission land grants to the politically connected.
1841	Receives, with brother Andrés, a 133,331-acre parcel, the present-day site of Camp Pendleton.
1845	Becomes Alta California governor for a second term; makes Los Angeles his capital.
1846	Flees to Mexico after US troops capture the territory.
1848	Becomes a US citizen with ratification of Treaty of Guadalupe Hidalgo; placed under house arrest for three weeks after returning to Los Angeles.
1852	Loses $1,600 in cash and 300 heads of cattle in one nine-mile horse race; sells his home to cover bets.
1870	Opens Southern California's finest hotel, the Pico House, fronting what would become L.A.'s downtown Plaza.
1880	Loses Pico House to foreclosure; goes bankrupt.
1893	Declines to attend Chicago World's Fair as "the last of the California dons;" tells organizers: "I do not intend to go to be one of the animals on display."
1894	Dies an American citizen in L.A. at the age of 93.

GANGS: A HISTORY

1920s	*Church football team in Boyle Heights Mexican immigrant community becomes White Fence, one of L.A.'s oldest gangs.*
1940s	*Calling themselves "Spook Hunters," white youths terrorize South L.A.'s growing black population.*
1942	*A grand jury indicts 17 suspected Mexican-American gang members for the death of Jose Gallardo Diaz in what becomes the "Sleepy Lagoon murder"; charges ultimately reversed on appeal.*
1972	*News reports describe gang members, strutting with canes, as "Crips."*
1984	*Rollin' 60s Crips kill four members of retired NFL player Kermit Alexander's family in a home invasion after misreading the address.*
1988	*The movie* Colors *premieres; gang brawls disrupt opening night.*
1989	*The term "gangster rap" first appears in Robert Hilburn's* Los Angeles Times *article on N.W.A.*
1992	*Drive-by shootings and homicides reach record highs.*
1992	*Crips and Bloods in Watts declare a truce the day before rioting erupts in response to Rodney King-LAPD verdict.*
1996	*Dr. Dre ends partnership with Death Row Records co-founder Suge Knight, relinquishing $50 million stake.*
2000	*LAPD disbands its anti-gang CRASH unit amid corruption charges that became known as the "Rampart Scandal."*
2001	*Father Gregory J. Boyle founds Homeboy Industries, one of the nation's largest and most successful gang rehabilitation programs.*
2004	*FBI launches the MS-13 National Gang Task Force aimed at L.A.-born, multinational Salvadoran gang Mara Salvatrucha.*
2005	*Stanley [Tookie] Williams III, a Crips founder and Nobel Peace Prize nominee, is executed at San Quentin State Prison.*
2015	*N.W.A biopic* Straight Outta Compton *is released.*
2016	*52 Mexican Mafia members arrested in $1.6 million drug bust near Corona.*
2016	*Suge Knight goes on trial for fatal hit-and-run outside Compton burger stand. Verdict pending.*

ZOOT SUIT RIOTS

In June 1943, heightened racial tensions in wartime Los Angeles culminated in a series of clashes between servicemen on leave and Mexican-Americans whose native garb they found offensive. Despite the brutality of these incidents, most press coverage was sympathetic to the servicemen. One exception was this account from Al Waxman, editor of the Jewish community newspaper *Eastside Journal.*

At Twelfth and Central I came upon a scene that will long live in my memory. Police were swinging clubs and servicemen were fighting with civilians. Wholesale arrests were being made by the officers.

Four boys came out of a pool hall...wearing the zoot-suits that have become the symbol of a fighting flag. Police ordered them into arrest cars. One refused. He asked: "Why am I being arrested?" The police officer answered with three swift blows of the night-stick across the boy's head and he went down. Police had difficulty loading his body into the vehicle because he was one-legged and wore a wooden limb.

At the next corner a Mexican mother cried out, "Don't take my boy, he did nothing. He's only fifteen years old." She was struck across the jaw with a night-stick and almost dropped the two and a half year old baby that was clinging in her arms...

Rushing back to the east side to make sure that things were quiet here, I came upon a band of servicemen making a tour of East First Street..."We're looking for zoot-suits to burn," they shouted. Again the police did not interfere.

Los Angeles Sunday Times
October 10, 1909

"NEW PLAYS WITHOUT WORDS ARE PUT ON FILMS HERE."

Southern California Conditions Found to Be Ideal for Moving Picture Work Because of Very Small Size of Negatives and Great Rapidity of Exposures — Real Actors in Demand for Pictures.

....

IF ANY ONE in Los Angeles or the neighboring country, particularly in the district about Edendale, should see a bunch of purported cowboys, Indians, bandits, cut-throats and robbers, riding or driving on the road or through the fields and up canyons and down gulches, he should not get frightened. It would not be necessary to rush into the house and get out the old rifle that his great grandfather used in the Revolutionary War or the old duck gun his great uncle carried while crossing the deserts...The wild and fantastic-looking people are nothing more than the Selig Polyscope Company's troupe out taking views for moving picture shows. The company has established a Pacific Coast branch at Eden-dale, and is now making half of its pictures in Southern California. The main headquarters of the company is in Chicago, where a city block is occupied. The company has bought the old Edendale Hall and two lots adjoining and is fitting up a temporary studio. Within a short time it will be able to develop and manufacture pictures in Los Angeles ready for theaters. "We have tried every part of the world," said Francis Boggs, who is general manager for the coast branch, "and we find that Los Angeles is the best place to make our pictures. Here we can find everything necessary for our outdoor work...most essential of all is the gorgeous sunlight. It is nearly as perfect as one can have for our work."

SANTA ANA WINDS

A fixture of legend, lore and literature, these desert-born hot, dry blusters are notorious for wreaking emotional and environmental havoc—making them perfect storytelling fodder, as revealed in the three references below.

"There was a desert wind blowing that night. It was one of those hot dry Santa Anas that come down through the mountain passes and curl your hair and make your nerves jump and your skin itch. On nights like that every booze party ends in a fight. Meek little wives feel the edge of the carving knife and study their husband's necks. Anything can happen. You can even get a full glass of beer at a cocktail lounge."

—Raymond Chandler, *Red Wind*

....

"There is something uneasy in the Los Angeles air this afternoon, some unnatural stillness, some tension. What it means is that tonight a Santa Ana will begin to blow, a hot wind from the northeast whining down through the Cajon and San Gorgonio Passes, blowing up sandstorms out along Route 66, drying the hills and the nerves to the flash point. For a few days now we will see smoke back in the canyons, and hear sirens at night. I have neither heard nor read that a Santa Ana is due, but I know it, and almost everyone I have seen today knows it too. We know it because we feel it. The baby frets. The maid sulks. I rekindle a waning argument with the telephone company, then cut my losses and lie down, given over to whatever is in the air."

—Joan Didion, *Los Angeles Notebook*

....

"It was a hot wind called the Santa Ana, and it carried with it the smell of warm places. It blew the strongest before dawn, across the Point. My friends and I would sleep in our cars, and the smell of the offshore wind would often wake us. And each morning, we knew this would be a special day."

—Robert Englund, *Big Wednesday*

MAPS

Illustrated maps of the city's quintessential bites,
outdoor adventure, local landmarks, classic movie theaters,
hidden stairways and the best of L.A. style.

EL MATADOR BEACH ROAD

CHANNEL ISLANDS

Malibu Creek State Park

BRIDGE
TO NOWHERE

ANGELES
CREST
Hwy →

↟↟↟↟↟↟↟↟ ↙
ANGELES
NATIONAL
FOREST ↟

THE
STRAND

LONG
BEACH

Santa Catalina
Island *

⇛ ADVENTURES ⇚

*With mountains to the east and ocean to the west, Angelenos
itching for exploration really do have it made in the sun.*

CATALINA ISLAND

Trek the Trans-Catalina Trail,
snorkel and free-dive at Italian
Gardens, kayak to hush-hush
beach campsites, and roam the
picturesque Avalon Harbor.
catalinabackcountry.com

EL MATADOR BEACH

Ten miles north of Malibu, El
Matador's pocket beach and
sea-stack rocks make for a rugged
sunset counter to the sandy
stretches down south. *32100
Pacific Coast Hwy*

THE STRAND

Fuel up at Brother's Burritos in
Hermosa, bike 15 miles north,
past Manhattan Beach, Marina
del Rey and the Z-Boys flow bowl
in Venice, then grab an ice cream
at Santa Monica Pier.
hermosacyclery.com

CHANNEL ISLANDS NATIONAL PARK

Seventy miles northwest of L.A.
proper, these five islands and
their treasured grottos, arches,
cliffs and caves are a sea kayaker's
dream. *islandkayaking.com*

BRIDGE TO NOWHERE

On this popular 10-mile hike,
ramblers ford the San Gabriel en
route to the abandoned 120-foot
arch bridge and a swimming
hole just beyond. Permits
required. *Camp Bonita Rd,
Angeles National Forest*

MALIBU CREEK STATE PARK

Over 8,000 acres of grassy trails
and canyon vistas, this sweeping
stretch of Santa Monica Mountains served as filming location
for *M*A*S*H* and others. *1925
Las Virgenes Rd*

ANGELES CREST HIGHWAY

Motorcyclists cruise this curvy
two-lane mountain road for
the most scenic, get-lost-for-a-
while escape from L.A. *66 miles,
La Cañada Flintridge to State
Hwy 138*

LOCAL EXPERT *Jedidiah Jenkins is executive editor of the
Los Angeles-based* Wilderness *magazine, which spotlights stories
about exploration, passion and grit.*

⋙ CLASSIC TASTES ⋘

From old-school tacos to off-menu pizza, these dishes have been nourishing the Angeleno soul for decades.

LANGER'S DELI
ORIGINAL #19
Langer's hand-carved pastrami on rye with coleslaw and Swiss is the only sandwich in town that won't start an argument. *704 S Alvarado St, langersdeli.com*

....

SPAGO
JEWISH PIZZA
Thin crust, smoked salmon, crème fraîche, caviar. And you still won't find it on Spago's menu. *176 N Canon Dr, wolfgangpuck.com*

....

ZANKOU CHICKEN
ROTISSERIE CHICKEN WITH GARLIC SPREAD
The white-hot garlic paste at the Armenian mini-chain may inspire more cravings than the fall-off-the-bone birds themselves. *5065 W Sunset Blvd, zankouchicken.com*

....

TITO'S
TITO'S TACO
In a city blessed with taco bounty, here the Mexican-American version is the gastronomic equivalent of an oldies soundtrack. *11222 Washington Pl, titostacos.com*

....

DAIKOKUYA
DAIKOKU RAMEN
The *kotteri*-style ramen—with extra back fat—keeps the lines long at Daikokuya's Little Tokyo flagship. *327 E 1st St, dkramen.com*

....

THE APPLE PAN
HICKORY BURGER
A bygone delight, daubed in a smoky-tangy sauce and served at a horseshoe counter by waiters in paper hats. *10801 W Pico Blvd*

....

PORTO'S BAKERY & CAFÉ
CHEESE ROLL
A pastry snatched up by the dozens is bound to inspire copycats—which is why Porto's trademarks their Cuban-style cheese roll. *315 N Brand Blvd, portosbakery.com*

LOCAL EXPERTS *For a taste of L.A.'s new classics, head to Animal, Son of a Gun or any of the other three restaurants run by visionary chefs Jon Shook and Vinny Dotolo.*

101

JEWISH PIZZA

BEVERLY *hills*

HICKORY BURGER

405

TITO'S TACO with CHEESE

CHEESE ROLL →

Glendale

ROTISSERIE CHICKEN with GARLIC

ORIGINAL #19

DAIKOKU RAMEN los ANGELES

Magic Castle

405

BEVERLY hills

10

10

HOLLYWOOD
FOREVER
CEMETERY

LAX

DOCKWEILER
FIRE PITS

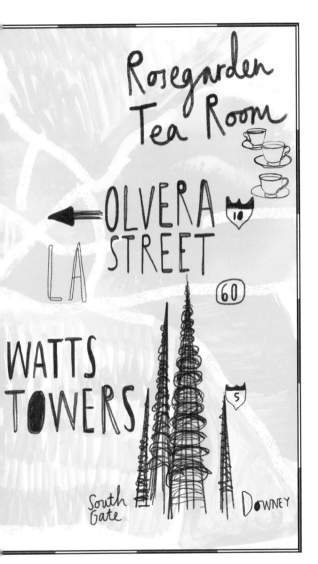

Rosegarden
Tea Room

OLVERA
STREET

10

60

LA

WATTS
TOWERS

5

South
Gate

Downey

»» LOCALS ONLY «««

Nobody wants to go look at handprints outside the Chinese Theatre with you, but your L.A. friends will happily play tourist if your list includes these landmarks.

OLVERA STREET

The site of an 18th-century Spanish pueblo, this is the city's true birthplace. Grab some taquitos at Cielito Lindo and see the lost Siqueiros mural. *845 N Alameda St, olvera-street.com*

MAGIC CASTLE

L.A.'s too hip for magic, unless it's in a boozy Victorian clubhouse in the Hollywood Hills. You'll need to dress up—and score an invite from a member of the Academy of Magical Arts. *7001 Franklin Ave, magiccastle.com*

WATTS TOWERS

This folk-art installation—an intricate cluster of spires assembled by artist Simon Rodia between 1921 and 1954—may be the city's greatest monument to the immigrant dream. *1727 E 107th St, wattstowers.us*

HOLLYWOOD FOREVER CEMETERY

Old Hollywood rests within the crypts and sarcophagi of this graveyard; al fresco movies, projected on a mausoleum wall, are a nocturnal picnic tradition. *6000 Santa Monica Blvd, hollywoodforever.com*

ROSE GARDEN TEA ROOM

Established in 1919 and encompassing 120 acres, the Huntington Library, Art Collections & Botanical Gardens in San Marino is the most civilized of escapes. *1151 Oxford Rd, huntington.org*

DOCKWEILER FIRE PITS

L.A. County spans 75 ocean-front miles, yet only one beach allows bonfires—assuming that you're lucky enough to nab one of Dockweiler's coveted fire rings. Remember that police still patrol for alcohol. *12001 Vista Del Mar, Playa del Rey, beaches.lacounty.gov*

LOCAL EXPERT *To expand your horizons, follow* @ChrisNicholsLA, *Los Angeles magazine's resident trivia hound and urban myth debunker.*

From Gothic to Beaux Arts, the old houses of the rapidly gentrifying Broadway corridor represent the nation's greatest concentration of historic theaters.

PALACE THEATRE [1911]
After decades as a second-run and Spanish-language movie venue, this vaudeville-era landmark survives as a special-event and filming locale. 630 *S Broadway, palacedowntown.com*

MILLION DOLLAR THEATRE [1918]
Created for impresario Sid Grauman, the Million Dollar was L.A.'s first grand movie palace. It has lived on as a jazz club, a Latin cabaret and a church. 307 *S Broadway, milliondollar.la*

STATE THEATRE [1921]
In its song-and-dance days, the State introduced the world to six-year-old Francis Gumm [later known, of course, as Judy Garland]. 703 *S Broadway, statetheater.la*

UNITED ARTISTS THEATRE [1927]
The house that United Artists [Charlie Chaplin, D.W. Griffith, Douglas Fairbanks and Mary Pickford] built, the theater now anchors the Ace Hotel. 933 *S Broadway, acehotel.com*

TOWER THEATRE [1927]
The first L.A. theater wired for sound—*The Jazz Singer* premiered here—the Tower is slated to become an Apple store. 802 *S Broadway, towertheatrela.com*

ORPHEUM THEATRE [1928]
Home to one of the few surviving Wurlitzer theater organs, and the most successfully restored of Broadway's anchors—as a recent filming of *American Idol* attests. 842 *S Broadway, laorpheum.com*

LOS ANGELES THEATRE [1931]
The last and most opulent of downtown's movie palaces, the Los Angeles opened its doors for the premiere of Charlie Chaplin's *City Lights*. 615 *S Broadway, losangelestheatre.com*

LOCAL EXPERT *Last Remaining Seats, the Los Angeles Conservancy's summer film series, is your best ticket to these magnificent cinemas.* laconservancy.org

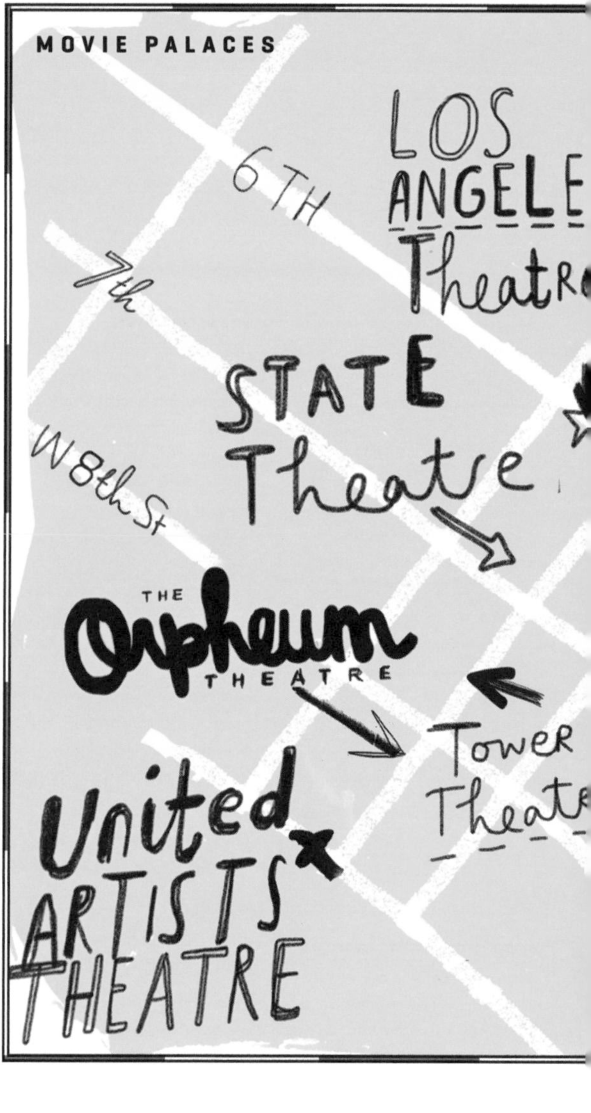

LOS ANGELES Theatre

6TH

7th

W 8th St

STATE Theatre

THE Orpheum THEATRE

TOWER Theatre

United ARTISTS THEATRE

Hill St.

S. BROADWAY

S. SPRING ST

Million Dollar Theatre

W. 3RD

Palace Theatre

6TH

7th

DOWNTOWN

POP CORN

POP CORN

BEACHWOOD Canyon

MUSIC BOX

Hollywood

BAXTER

Los ANGELES

CULVER CITY

Huntington Park

⇒ SECRET STAIRS ⇐

Before L.A. surrendered to the car, stairways connected hillside communities to trolley lines. These secluded steps are so popular today, people drive to them.

MUSIC BOX

In their Oscar-winning short, *The Music Box*, Stan Laurel and Oliver Hardy wrestled a piano up this flight of 133 steps in Silver Lake. Well, here's another nice mess you've gotten us into, fellas. *923-925 N Vendome St*

....

BAXTER

The 231 steps zigzagging across this vertiginous Echo Park slope get steeper as they ascend, but the downtown panoramas at the top are worth it. Sunset Instagramming recommended. *1501 Baxter St*

....

BEACHWOOD CANYON

In the community originally known as Hollywoodland, an 861-step network of staircases, most of them cut from granite, links canyon streets. *2800 Beachwood Dr*

CULVER CITY

Officially known as the Baldwin Hills Scenic Overlook, these 282 irregularly shaped risers, formed from recycled concrete, lead to a decommissioned hilltop reservoir. Record sprint up is two minutes, nine seconds. *6300 Hetzler Rd*

....

SANTA MONICA

These twin staircases—one wooden [170 steps], one concrete [199 steps]—have turned Santa Monica Canyon into the sceniest workout in town. *4th St and Adelaide Dr*

....

CASTELLAMMARE

Rising from PCH, this 518-step chain of staircases snakes up and down a landslide-prone bluff in Pacific Palisades, offering ocean views at every turn. End your hike on the beach. *Breve Way and Castellammare Dr*

LOCAL EXPERT *Nobody has done more to rediscover L.A.'s stairways than Charles Fleming, whose book* Secret Stairs: A Walking Guide to the Historic Staircases of Los Angeles *is the essential primer.*

⋙ STYLE ⋘

*With its modern mercantiles, bohemian boutiques and vintage
savants, L.A.'s style scene is continually reshaping the global vibe.*

TRADING POST

Vintage inspiration filled
with denim, small-batch accessories, household sundries, plus
their own apparel line, Dr. Collectors. *177 S La Brea Ave,
tradingpostla.com*

RTH

Hit up these cozy, cultishly
revered stores for the global
selection of designer clothing, accessories and leather
goods. *537 N La Cienega Blvd,
rthshop.com*

MOHAWK GENERAL STORE

Silver Lake's modernist
den feels like Amsterdam,
but sunnier, with smart
clothing, objects, furniture,
lamps and books. *4011 W Sunset
Blvd, mohawkgeneralstore.com*

GENERAL QUARTERS

Owner Blair Lucio's penchant
for SoCal heritage brands and
attention to 360° service [e.g. the
in-house '50s-style barbershop]
lures in fellas whether they need
new threads or not. *153 S La Brea
Ave, generalquartersstore.com*

LCD

Every inch of this 600-square-
foot Venice women's boutique is
packed with modern and minimalist clothing, accessories,
jewelry, beauty and home goods.
1919 Lincoln Blvd, shoplcd.co/

GENTLEMAN'S BREAKFAST

Housed in former garage off
Sunset, this Echo Park optical
shop hawks vintage shades and
pours free Scotch. *1101 Mohawk
St, gentsbreakfast.blogspot.com*

AMERICAN RAG

Launched to acclaim in the early
1980s by visionary Mark Verts, this
10,000-square-foot emporium is
both a nostalgic vintage trove and
a new wave outpost for fashion
designers. *150 S La Brea Ave,
americanrag.com*

LOCAL EXPERTS *Raan and Lindsay Parton [Apolis and
Alchemy Works] anchor DTLA's Arts District with a contemporary
sensibility for home and fashion.* 806 and 826 E 3rd St

BEL AIR

HOLLYWOO

RTH
SHOP

Beverly Hills

GENERAL
Quarters

LCD

Culver
City

10

405

Glendale

MOHAWK GENERAL STORE

GENTLEMENS BREAKFAST

WEST Hollywood

echo Park

AMERICAN RAG

TRADING POST

Los ANGELES downtown

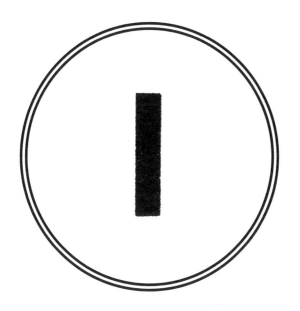

INTERVIEWS

Fourteen conversations with locals of note about lifeguards, food writing, native plants, punk rock, casting a movie, L.A. gang culture and more

NANCY SILVERTON

CHEF AND RESTAURATEUR

STANDING IN THE dormitory kitchen at Sonoma State, all that stainless steel, I remember thinking, "Wow. I want to do this for the rest of my life."

I DIDN'T WANT to be on TV or have a thousand restaurants or any of that. I just wanted to cook.

I GREW UP in the San Fernando Valley, and I loved Swanson TV dinners.

NOBODY—including Wolfgang Puck—had any idea about what Spago was going to become.

WHAT IF I open that door and nobody comes? That's the fear.

WHERE PEOPLE SAT, the waiting list, the who's who. How Wolfgang danced around that was really something.

WITH BREAD, fundamentally, you're dealing with something alive.

ONCE YOU REALIZE you can't control what you're doing, it starts to work. It's like parenting.

A GRILLED GRUYÈRE sandwich. That is one of the best things in the world.

I LOVE THE PIZZA in Rome. A long slab, cut into squares, minimal ingredients. That's what inspired Mozza.

I WAS VERY concerned about the crust.

EVEN WITH THE James Beard Award, I don't feel like that kind of chef. I still feel like the baker.

A LOT OF COOKS feel the need to complicate their food with ingredients and equipment. For me, the tools are pots and pans and whisks and wooden spoons and a wood-fire grill.

BUT I KNOW what makes a dish a dish. I know how to edit.

AND I STILL get the adrenaline rush when tickets start coming into the kitchen.

≫ ED YU ≪

TRAFFIC EXPERT

DURING THE 1984 Olympics, we couldn't widen the streets, so we had to create a system to improve the efficiency of the intersections and a way to view it all in real time, from one central location.

PEOPLE ALWAYS describe it as mission control. Like *Star Trek*.

THERE ARE 7,000 miles of public streets, and every signal in the city—4,600-plus—is hardwired.

WE HAVE ABOUT 550 cameras scattered around. I can see 12 to 18 intersections at once.

TRAFFIC IS LIKE WATER. You stop it one way, it's gonna flow another way.

THE BUSES receive priority.

LET'S SAY A BUS is going down this street, and it's behind schedule. Our system will recognize that, and it will add time to the intersection ahead so it can get back on schedule.

IN CERTAIN AREAS, there are special horse push-buttons, placed at a rider's height to allow them to cross on the horse trails.

HOLLYWOOD and Highland is probably one of the most problematic intersections we have—cars, lots of pedestrians, tour buses and premieres.

I'VE LIVED IN L.A. all my life. The transportation culture has changed a lot.

IN THE 1990s I wouldn't have had a pedestrian being run over because they were on their cell phone crossing the street. Now it happens a lot.

AS A DRIVER, you have to be Zen.

IF YOU LIVE HERE long enough, you know that's just the way it is. You just turn up the music and keep on going.

ESPERANZA RISKIN

INSTRUMENT SHOP OWNER

MY HUSBAND, Bob, was the first to get involved with McCabe's.

A FRIEND OF HIS family found an old guitar in the attic, a 1914 Martin, so he brought it into the shop to be repaired.

WALTER CAMP, McCabe's co-owner at the time, said, "I don't have time to fix it now, but I'll show you how."

BOB BECAME the official luthier and never left.

WE'LL CELEBRATE our 60th anniversary in 2018.

MCCABE'S is known for our weekly concerts.

DOC WATSON, Jackson Browne, Allen Ginsberg, the comedian Mort Sahl, Bonnie Raitt, Ry Cooder, even the Spinal Tap guys—every kind of artist has performed here.

WE WERE ONE of the first, if not the first, Taylor dealerships in L.A.

THEY TREATED our manager at the time as a one-man focus group.

AND, WE CONVERTED a Martin into a 12-string before Martin had a 12-string.

EVERYONE who works here is a musician.

ONE OF OUR GUYS, who buys books for us and writes for the website, plays bass for Mavis Staples.

I DON'T KNOW how much guitar string we've sold—more than 1,000 miles for sure. Add in the other stringed instruments, and the length could probably circumnavigate the world.

INSTRUMENT INTEREST goes in waves. Right now, it's ukuleles and electric sitars.

OUR MANTRA has always been an open invitation: "Rentals for the cautious, lessons for the eager, truth-telling for the fearful, repairs for the clumsy, concerts for the devoted and a free pick and coffee for all."

⫸ DICK METZ ⫷

SURF LEGEND

THE ENDLESS SUMMER was made about a surfing trip I took around the world.

....

WHEN I GOT BACK, I showed the slides I'd been taking to Bruce Brown, then talked him into following my trip.

....

BRUCE DID IT in an airplane in six weeks. It took me three years.

....

I DIDN'T FLY AT ALL. I got jobs on ships, and then I hitchhiked.

....

WHEN I WAS A KID, my dad owned a railroad-car restaurant on the beach called the Laguna Diner. He'd put me under the lifeguard tower in a playpen so he could be cooking hamburgers and still see me.

....

AT THE TIME, Peanuts Larson and his schoolmate, a guy named Hevs McClelland, lived on the beach and didn't have jobs.

....

MY DAD TOLD THEM, "Watch my kid and I'll give you a beer and a hamburger at the end of the day."

....

THEY HAD A Ford Model A coupe. They'd put their boards in the rumble seat and me in the back and go to Doheny or San Onofre to surf.

....

THEY DIDN'T REALLY give a shit about me, but I was their meal ticket.

....

NOW MOTORCYCLING is my favorite sport. I race dirt bikes in the summertime, up in the mountains, every day I can.

....

I BOUGHT MY FIRST motorcycle when I was 60, so it's a new sport for me. I feel like I'm still getting better instead of worse.

....

I STILL SURF, but it's harder for me to get up quick enough.

....

I'VE SURFED ALL MY LIFE, and I've surfed all over the world. So I've kind of done it all. I'm satisfied with surfing.

》 MISTER CARTOON 《

TATTOO ARTIST

MY PARENTS NAMED ME after a saint, Saint Marcos.

TATTOOING IS as close to spiritual as I get.

I GREW UP in the Harbor area of Los Angeles, down by the water near the docks.

MOST YOUNG GUYS there dream of being a longshoreman or a drug dealer—in either case it's a lot of money for not a lot of work.

I DIDN'T FIT into either one of those categories.

MY PARENTS were both creative people. They had a small mom-and-pop print shop, where they made posters and restaurant menus and business cards. Gold foil, embossing, custom stuff.

I STARTED DRAWING as a little boy. By the time I was eight or nine, the local newspaper ran its first story on me as an artist.

MY DAD TOOK ME to car shows as a kid, and I would see the local airbrush guy putting portraits on cars and names on T-shirts. That seemed pretty cool.

THE FIRST DAY I airbrushed T-shirts, I made $1,000.

I WAS DOING IT at car shows and swap meets.

WE WOULD BUY white T-shirts and airbrush them with names: of our neighborhoods, our crews, our girls, whatever we could do to make it custom. It was the precursor to streetwear, which didn't exist when I was growing up.

I STARTED TATTOOING professionally when I was 24, which is pretty old.

I MIMICKED the artists who sent their designs to my parents' print shop.

I TRIED TO DRAW things that were real and that people could identify with.

BACK THEN, tattoo shops were really raw. It wasn't uncommon on a Saturday night to see a rich guy with a stupid idea get a foot in his ass.

WE USED TO MAKE our own needles with a solder gun and send them out to be sterilized by a place that worked with local dentists.

NOW YOU HAVE GUYS coming from art school talking about photorealism and shit, opening tattoo shops. More like boutiques, really.

AND EVERYTHING is disposable.

SKIN CANVAS is different than any other canvas. It's not flat like paper or porous in the same way a wall or the hood of a car is.

MY STYLE IS old-school Chicano fine line mixed with graffiti art mixed with graphic design and commercial signage-type letters.

THE PRICE RANGES from person to person. A sleeve or stomach rocker takes multiple sessions. Your name in script—in and out in an hour.

REGARDLESS of what I charge you, though, you're going to have this tattoo for longer than I'm going to have your money.

THE LONGEST I've ever worked on a tattoo? Ten hours. Way too long. They're dying at the end of it, and I'm tired as hell. Now I try not to tattoo over 5 to 6 hours.

IT'S A SAFE, comfortable environment. I got Fiji waters, some healthy Clif Bars, some Halloween candy laid out. You want a latte? No problem.

IF PEOPLE PASS OUT during the session, it's not because of the tattoo. It's the anticipation of the pain.

A SIX-FOUR, 280-POUND guy might be struggling hard, but I've had 100-pound Japanese girls get full sleeves and not flinch. It's all in your mind.

EVEN THOUGH I'm successful, I'm not above my roots.

IF MY DAUGHTERS are going to a Selena Gomez concert, I airbrush a T-shirt for them. I'm still the kid at the swap meet, and that will never change.

⟫ T. RODGERS ⟪

FORMER GANG LEADER

I'VE GROWN TO DESPISE the term "OG." It's a colloquialism now. I worked blood, sweat and tears to get that title.

IT CAME with a lot of things, including imprisonment.

AS A YOUNG MAN, I didn't think I would live this long.

I WOULD WALK out my house and look down the alleyway, and in that alley was diamonds, rubies, pearls, gold, platinum—it was broken glass, discarded wine bottles, but in my mind it was a treasure trove. I was the prince of that alley.

I WAS NEVER a robber, never took nothing from anybody. If I didn't have the gift of gab for a motherfucker to give it to me, then it wasn't for me to have.

T. RODGERS IS compassionate, he is empathetic, he is understanding, he is charismatic—he is a gentleman and a gangster.

I TOLD THE POLICE ONCE, if your ass is smart enough to catch me and I'm stupid enough to allow you to catch me, then I mean to be in prison.

I DIDN'T GO to the penitentiary until I was in my 50s.

I DON'T HAVE a neighborhood. We have a proliferation of young white people moving in, buying up the properties. Gentrification, plain and simple.

I HAVE ALL THE THINGS I need. I have nothing I want.

DRIVING FOR UBER was the greatest cyber-pimping I've ever experienced. They really push for you to get out there and sell your ass.

A TELLER OF TRUTH has no friends.

LOVE. TRUTH. PEACE. Freedom. Justice. Never deviated from the five principles. I think that's what made me a sort of nontraditional leader. There was a foundation I believed in.

⟫ ALICE BAG ⟪

PUNK MUSICIAN

I WAS BORN and raised in East L.A.

FROM MY KITCHEN window I can see the downtown skyline, and the dirty air paints beautiful sunsets.

L.A. IS A COSMOPOLITAN city. To get the most juice out of that orange, it helps to be bi- or multilingual.

THE EARLY HOLLYWOOD punk scene was created by a wide variety of kooks, including people of color, women and queers.

WE USED TO HANG OUT at The Masque, a bomb shelter under The Pussycat Theater near Cherokee and Hollywood Boulevard.

BRICKTOPS was a '20s-style speakeasy in West Hollywood that was run by my friend, Vaginal Davis. She has since moved to Berlin.

WHEN I PASS BY the building, I sometimes get a feeling of longing for Bricktops, but I think I just miss Vaginal Davis.

BEING ONSTAGE makes me feel fearless and bold.

SOME OF THE most exciting shows I've performed at have been at rundown, hole-in-the-wall venues.

I'LL TAKE A PLACE with a sense of community over a place with an expensive sound system any day.

I STILL ENJOY going to shows, but I don't party every night anymore.

I LISTEN TO MUSIC at home, in the car, at clubs, tire shops, record stores, rented halls, community centers, wherever it's happening.

I REALLY LIKE FEA and The Sex Stains. There's also a band from Fresno called Fatty Cakes and the Puff Pastries that makes me want to dance and eat!

⫸ JENNIFER BENDER ⫷

CASTING EXECUTIVE

THERE REALLY IS a Central Casting. It goes back to the early years of Hollywood, when actors were just going from studio to studio, literally waving at the front gates to see if they could get hired. It was a bit chaotic, so the studios came together in 1925 and created Central Casting Corp.

IT'S FUN TO CONNECT this commonly used phrase to an actual place that's been around 90 years.

I WAS ON JURY DUTY several years ago and the judge was asking questions, trying to weed out who's who. I said I work in the entertainment business. And the judge is like, "OK, what do you do?" And I said, "I'm in casting." He was trying to get more specifics out of me, and jokingly he said, "What, do you work at Central Casting or something?"

WE'RE A LITTLE gateway into Hollywood. If you come to Central Casting, as cliché as it sounds, you could become a star.

NOT THAT WE directly get people into their big break, but quite a few people got their career started doing background work. The most famous one is Brad Pitt.

MONDAY, WEDNESDAY, Friday: anyone can come in. It's free to sign up.

WE ARE THE LARGEST employment agency in California.

MOST BUSINESSES, you can't hire people based on how they look. We're the opposite of that.

IT'S NOT TO SAY we're only looking for pretty people. It could be zombies. It could be futuristic aliens.

MANY PEOPLE come here, they've just arrived in L.A. Some, like, drove in that morning, and that afternoon have been sent out on a set.

YOU ARE THERE to work. You're not there to get so-and-so's autograph.

⫸ SHAMELL BELL ⫷

ACTIVIST AND CHOREOGRAPHER

I GREW UP Section 8 in South-Central Los Angeles.

ART CAN SAVE LIVES. I know that because I have a very different life than my brother.

MY MOM fought for me to get in a performing arts magnet school. It was an hour-long bus ride.

WE'RE BLACK and we're young and we're in Los Angeles and we're dancing in the street, so they're going to assume we are doing something criminal.

CAN YOU AUDITION for Will Smith? They need a krumper.

KRUMPING is fast-paced arm movements. It's aggressive. Jerkin' is a mix of breakdancing and the Hoover Stomp. It's very acrobatic.

YOUR VISION and your talent? That thing is your purpose.

DANCE CAN BE a disruption. It's a tactic to stop people and make them feel something.

TRAYVON MARTIN started my activism. It became about all the Trayvons.

DR. MELINA ABDULLAH is a spiritual mom to me.

HE HAD SKITTLES and an iced tea, talking to a girl on the phone, walking in his dad's neighborhood, and he's dead. What can we do?

GO TO THE STREETS, she said.

THAT BECAME the first chapter of Black Lives Matter-LA.

IT IS OUR DUTY to fight for freedom. It is our duty to win. We must love and protect one another. We have nothing to lose but our chains.

MY SON has been leading the chant since he was two.

COPS ARE NOT BAD people. The training, the implicit bias, a system built on superiority and disadvantage—that's the problem.

»» JONATHAN GOLD ««

FOOD WRITER AND CRITIC

I'M MORE or less a completist. I'll eat everywhere.

WHEN I WAS right out of UCLA, almost as something to do, I decided that I was going to eat at every restaurant on Pico Boulevard, where I lived at the time, starting at a Salvadoran restaurant near the Coca-Cola Building all the way down to the curly fries stand at the beach.

MY MOST RECENT attempt was to go to every restaurant in the San Gabriel Valley that had the word "tasty" in its name.

I EAT OUT 10 meals a week.

MY JOB IS ACTUALLY physically taxing.

I GO TO THE GYM five times a week and still look like this!

I DON'T KEEP any restaurants to myself if I think they're great.

BUT IF THERE ARE 14 places serving a certain kind of dumpling, I don't feel it necessary to tell people about all 14.

ONE OF THE GREAT things about L.A. is you can decide that you want to eat, essentially, as if you live in Guadalajara. Or you can decide you want to eat, essentially, as if you're in Chengdu.

I'M NOT QUITE at the level where I can Instagram a place and it will become mobbed.

BUT I CAN DO a paragraph on a place and it'll end up being mobbed.

THAT'S DEFINITELY ONE of the benefits of the job.

I WRITE ABOUT a place, somebody goes there, they're happy, and then they associate their happiness with me.

THE CITY is huge.

I LEARN EVERY DAY that there is always something that you don't know in Los Angeles.

⫸ SETH RILEY ⫷

WILDLIFE ECOLOGIST

IF ANY GROUP is going to be affected by habitat loss and fragmentation, it would be carnivores.

CARNIVORES need a huge amount of space.

WE HAVE SOME challenges here at the Santa Monica Mountains National Recreation Area, being within the second-largest metropolitan area in the country.

LOS ANGELES is a megacity, and there's maybe one other in the world that has a large cat in it, specifically, Mumbai with its leopards.

WE STARTED studying bobcats 20 years ago. We studied coyotes intensively for quite a long time, and we've been studying mountain lions since 2002.

IT'S AN AMAZING thing that in 2017 we still have mountain lions roaming one of the biggest cities in the world.

WE CALL THEM "mountain lions," typically. In the Southwest they say "puma," and in the Northwest they say "cougar."

THEY'RE PRETTY amazing animals. They're deer specialists, so they live by taking down an animal bigger than they are.

WE DO NOT name the animals like you would a pet.

YOU GET ATTACHED to them anyway, so if one that's named after your friend gets run over by a car on the freeway or dies of rodenticide poisoning, that's sort of a bummer.

WE'RE EXCITED by possibly creating a wildlife crossing over the 101.

IT'S EIGHT lanes of traffic!

EVERYONE WHO DRIVES along that stretch would see that giant overpass and know that Southern California cares a lot about wildlife and preserving wild places.

»» NICK HUMMINGBIRD ««

NATIVE PLANTS

MY LEGAL LAST NAME is Hernandez. A lot of people say, "Hey, that's a Spanish name, not an Indian name."

....

THEY DON'T REALIZE that we were colonized by Spaniards and the missions here.

....

I USED TO BE a law enforcement ranger at Joshua Tree National Park.

....

PEOPLE WERE DOING stupid things, and I wanted to make a change.

....

ONE OFFICER cannot police 10,000 people.

....

IT'S TAKEN A LOT of positive energy to make my plant nursery, Hahamonga, what it is.

....

I KNOW THE TONGVA ancestors who were here over the thousands of years are happy with that.

....

AND IT'S IMPORTANT for people to know that Indians are still here. We will always be here.

....

OUR DISPLACEMENT, which took us away from our caretaker role, has really hurt the environment.

....

THE HEALTH of the land was *our* health.

....

OAKS PROVIDED carbohydrate sustenance in the form of acorns in a time we needed it most, in the fall, to prepare for the cold winters ahead.

....

WHEN A WOMAN in our culture had a child, she would usually go out alone, dig a hole and plant the afterbirth with an acorn.

....

IT TIED THAT CHILD to a plant that would one day grow into a huge oak tree and ensured that there was life for those to come. Not just for humans but for squirrels, scrub jays, woodpeckers, deer.

....

IT'S HARD TO SEE the destruction of these oak trees. Those are our ancestors.

ARTHUR VERGE

VETERAN LIFEGUARD

I GREW UP in Santa Monica, and I spent 42 years as an L.A. County lifeguard.

MY GREAT-GRANDMOTHER was a true Californio. She worked as a midwife in the Pacific Palisades.

HER DAUGHTER, Maria, married my grandfather, Arthur Verge. He was French Canadian.

HE WAS THE ATTORNEY for the gambling ships out in Santa Monica Bay.

I REMEMBER BEING a kid and my parents taking me to the gangster Mickey Cohen's ice cream shop in Brentwood Country Mart.

MY FATHER put himself through college by lifeguarding.

L.A. HIRED the first lifeguards in the 1920s from the pools.

THEY'D GIVE THEM a little metal rescue can and tell them, "Make sure nobody drowns."

GEORGE WOLFE RODE a bike up and down the Venice Boardwalk. Cat Watkins, whose father had been an Indian fighter, would take a horse and patrol Santa Monica.

WHEN THE Great Depression hit, everyone was going to the beach. They weren't working.

IT'S BEEN THE SAME basic test, I'd say, since 1931.

A 200-METER RUN to the ocean, 1,000-meter swim to the buoy, then 200-meter run up the beach.

THE TOP 50 are hired.

IF YOU SWIM 1,000 yards in under 12 minutes, you're going to make it.

THE SQUAD is 125 full-time. The rest of the pool—part-time lifeguard —is about 700.

WE COVER 72 MILES, Ventura to Long Beach, including Catalina.

EGO IS NOT ALLOWED. As they say: No tall poppies.

TWO YEARS AGO, we had everything go wrong. Shark attack on the Manhattan Beach Pier. Lightning strikes at Venice Beach. It was full-on triage.

I CALL IT command presence. "Everything is OK. Stop it. Calm down." It's the voice from God.

RIP CURRENTS cause 80 percent of our rescues.

TELLING SOMEONE to not panic, to let it take you, then swim parallel to shore sounds great on paper.

IN 2014, Ben Carlson was a lifeguard in Newport Beach, and he went after an obese man. They went over a huge wave, and Ben crashed to the bottom and he drowned.

A FEW WEEKS LATER, one of the younger guards—a big, tough, rugged guy—came up to me and told me about getting thrown to the bottom on a rescue.

"I GOT A WIFE and two kids," he told me. "And I couldn't stop thinking of Ben."

TO ME, THE AVENUES at Venice is the hardest to work. One summer we had 1,200 rescues there. I lost 11 pounds.

NEVER TURN your back on the water. When you least expect it, expect it. When in doubt, go out.

THOSE ARE MY THREE cardinal rules.

IN ALL, THE SHOW *Baywatch* was great for us. Raised awareness for the guards. My friend Greg co-created it.

BUT WE WOULD ROAR at some things they did on the show. We gave Greg holy crap for it.

A BLITZ IS WHEN more than three people are caught in a rip.

ONE DAY there were 14 people out in the rip. My friend drove over in the truck, jumped out, and forgot to put it in Park.

NEXT THING YOU KNOW, the truck is out in the water, crashing against the pier. People were cheering.

THAT ANECDOTE ended up on TV.

»» LUIS J. RODRIGUEZ ««

POET

THERE'S SO MUCH poetry in Los Angeles.

PEOPLE COME HERE for the big Hollywood dream, whatever it is. Underneath is a lot of pain, a lot of poverty, a lot of hurt.

LOS ANGELES IS ALSO the end of the line. The Ocean.

BEING POET LAUREATE was the opportunity to not just bring poetry to as many places as possible, but to draw it out of the community.

THE FIRST YEAR they wanted me to do a minimum six events. I did 110.

I WAS A PRETTY troubled kid. And pretty murderous. Until books spoke to me.

THE LIBRARY was my refuge. Books gave me the idea of what was possible.

THERE'S A LOT OF sociological studies about Chicano gangs. I think I might be the first actual gang participant that wrote a book about their experience.

IT'S ONE OF the most checked-out books. There was a time that it was also the most stolen.

IF YOU'RE GOING TO steal anything, steal a book, and if you're going to steal a book, steal my book.

LANGUAGE IS USED to inform you, persuade you, or sell you something.

YOU NEED an imagination before you can make a turn.

I RAN FOR governor in 2014.

I WENT UP AND DOWN the state 12 times with no money—well, $27,000. In the end, I got 67,000 votes.

THE FUNNY THING: I won second in San Francisco after Governor Brown. And in the border communities, I was number one. It was quite amazing, considering I was really nobody.

ESSAYS

Original stories from two celebrated local writers, excerpts from
11 iconic film reviews and a retrospective on the Pulitzer-winning
coverage of the 1992 riots by the Los Angeles Times *staff*

⇾ ON FILM ⇽

*An original voice. Vigorous opinions. And, above
all, the willingness to be transfixed every time the lights
go down. The best-of-the-best film critics bring these
qualities, and more, to every review they share with
the cinematic world. Below are brief excerpts
from critiques of 11 landmark films.*

SUNSET BOULEVARD

Thomas M. Pryor
The New York Times
August 11, 1950

A segment of life in Hollywood is being spread across the screen of the Music Hall in *Sunset Boulevard*. Using as the basis of their frank, caustic drama a scandalous situation involving a faded, aging silent screen star and a penniless, cynical young scriptwriter, Charles Brackett and Billy Wilder [with an assist from D. M. Marshman, Jr.] have written a powerful story of the ambitions and frustrations that combine to make life in the cardboard city so fascinating to the outside world.

Gloria Swanson was coaxed out of long retirement to portray the pathetic, forgotten film queen, Norma Desmond, and now it can be said that it is inconceivable that anyone else might have been considered for the role. With uncommon skill, Brackett and Wilder, who also produced and directed this splendid drama for Paramount

Pictures, have kept an essentially tawdry romance from becoming distasteful and embarrassing. Aside from the natural, knowing tone of the dialogue, the realism of the picture is heightened by scenes set inside the actual iron-grilled gates of the Paramount Studio, where Norma Desmond goes for an on-the-set visit with her old comrade, Cecil B. DeMille himself. And the fantastic, Babylonian atmosphere of an incredible past is reflected sharply in the gaudy elegance of the decaying mansion in which Norma Desmond lives.

REBEL WITHOUT A CAUSE

Robert J. Landry
Variety
October 26, 1955

Here is a fairly exciting, suspenseful and provocative, if also occasionally far-fetched, melodrama of unhappy youth on another delinquency kick. The plot bears no resemblance to the content of a book of the same title published a few years ago. The book was a clinical study of a withdrawn boy. The film presents a boy whose rebellion against a weakling father and a shrewish mother expresses itself in boozing, knife-fighting and other forms of physical combat and testing of his own manhood.

The performance of the star, James Dean, will excite discussion, especially in connection with the irony of his own recent crash death under real-life conditions of recklessness which form a macabre pressagent frame as the picture goes into release. In *East of Eden*, under Elia Kazan's direction, the 24-year-old actor was widely thought to be doing a Marlon Brando. But freed from Kazan's evaluations of character, this resemblance vanishes. Almost free of mannerisms under [Director Nicholas] Ray's pacing, Dean is very effective as a boy groping for adjustment to people. As a "farewell" performance he leaves behind, with this film, genuine artistic regret, for here was a talent which might have touched the heights. His actor's capacity to get inside the skin of youthful pain, torment and bewilderment is not often encountered.

CHINATOWN

Vincent Canby
The New York Times
June 21, 1974

Pin-striped suits, men's hair parted slightly off-center like Richard Arlen's, four-door convertible touring cars [not yet declared unsafe], official portraits of Franklin D. Roosevelt in public buildings, women with marceled hair, and elegant slouches.

These are just some of the 1930's artifacts that decorate Roman Polanski's *Chinatown*, a new private-eye melodrama that celebrates not only a time and a place [Los Angeles] but also a kind of criminality that to us jaded souls today appears to be nothing worse than an eccentric form of legitimate private enterprise.

In that far-off time—midway between the repeal of Prohibition and the inauguration of lend-lease—murderers, swindlers, and blackmailers acted according to carefully premeditated plans. These plans, in turn, were always there for the uncovering by a Sam Spade or a Philip Marlowe or, in this case, a J. J. Gittes, a man whose name is repeatedly mispronounced as Gibbs, which is one of the burdens he learns to live with, along with a vulnerable nose.

The plot is a labyrinth of successive revelations having to do with Los Angeles water reserves, land rights, fraud, and intra-family hankypanky, climaxing in Los Angeles's Chinatown on a street that seems no more mysterious than Flatbush Avenue.

STAR WARS

Pauline Kael
The New Yorker
September 26, 1977

Star Wars is like getting a box of Cracker Jack which is all prizes. This is the writer-director George Lucas's own film, subject to no business interference, yet it's a film that's totally uninterested in anything that doesn't connect with the mass audience. There's no breather in the picture, no lyricism; the only attempt at beauty is in the double sunset. It's enjoyable on its own terms, but it's exhausting, too: like taking a pack of kids to the circus. An hour into it, children say that they're ready to see it again; that's because it's an assemblage of spare parts—it has no emotional grip. *Star Wars* may be the only movie in which the first time around the surprises are reassuring.... It's an epic without a dream. But it's probably the absence of wonder that accounts for the film's special, huge success. The excitement of those who call it the film of the year goes way past nostalgia to the feeling that now is the time to return to childhood.

E.T.—THE EXTRA-TERRESTRIAL

Todd McCarthy
Variety
May 26, 1982

E.T.—the Extra-Terrestrial may be the best Disney film Disney never made. Captivating, endearingly optimistic and magical at times, Steven Spielberg's fantasy about a stranded alien from outer space protected by three kids until it can arrange for passage home is certain to capture the imagination of the world's youth in the manner of most of his earlier pics, as well as those of George Lucas. The result will be a summertime bonanza for Universal Studios.

The opening sequence actually comes off like a repeat of *Close Encounters*'s final frames, as a sizeable spaceship takes off just before some earthly authorities are able to close in on it. One of its occupants gets left behind, however, and the viewer is instantly sympathetic with its plight in the threateningly different environment of a modern California subdivision.

Rarely has a picture so completely evinced a kid's point of view and shown the complicity of youngsters against adults. It's been said that the only people who don't like Disneyland are late-adolescents who feel too hip to enjoy the pleasures of their earlier years, and the same will probably hold true for *E.T.*

Chalk up another smash for Spielberg.

DIE HARD

Richard Schickel
Time
July 25, 1988

Bruce Willis has based his career on apologizing for being a man. Robert De Niro has based his on not apologizing for being an actor. Neither characteristic necessarily qualifies a man to play the lead in an action movie. But when the bullets are flying, the pyrotechnics are booming and everyone is ankle-deep in broken glass, the guy who knows how to play charm is bound to look disadvantaged next to the one who knows how to play roles.

In the first half of director John McTiernan's movie, Willis wears an undershirt. In the second half he gets rid of it. And that's pretty much it for his performance. Of course, an actor is hard pressed to create a characterization when all he has to play against is gunshots and explosions. And any actor deserves sympathy when his love interest is sequestered from him, his nemeses are without human interest, his potential allies are all idiots and the only sensible figure on the scene [Reginald VelJohnson] is always a walkie-talkie away.

Good, bad or indifferent, megabangs are beginning to cost megabucks. Reportedly, each of these films costs well over $30 million, with De Niro and Willis pulling in about $5 million a head. And in a season in which Schwarzenegger's *Red Heat* and Sylvester Stallone's pricey *Rambo III* are having trouble reaching profit, scholars of the bottom line are wondering if the action-adventure genre has a future. Possibly not, if people keep putting their money into more noise and bigger flames.

BOYZ N THE HOOD

Todd McCarthy
Variety
May 20, 1991

If *Do The Right Thing* hadn't already been used, it would have been the best title for *Boyz N The Hood*, an absorbing, smartly made dramatic encyclopedia of problems and ethics in the black community, 1991. An impressive debut by 23-year-old writer-director John Singleton, it is a sincere pic [that] clearly knows whereof it speaks and does so from an enlightened point of view that will command critical respect and generate good b.o.

The tale principally looks at the lives of three boys in South-Central L.A., beginning in '84 and then jumping, after a half-hour, to the present, when the realities of violence hit the teens.

Along the way, however, a rich tapestry of diverse characters is painted, as is a picture of how much strength is required to break out of old patterns and change lives in a positive way.

Singleton constantly and effectively lays in the irritants and reminders of violence in the 'hood—the jets and choppers flying overhead, the everpresent dense smog, the random, easily provoked fights, the day-and-night wailing of police sirens, the nearby gunshots—all of which echo the opening title stating that one in 21 black males will end up murdered.

SWINGERS

Janet Maslin
The New York Times
October 18, 1996

Mr. Favreau's very funny, self-deprecating screenplay isn't about much more than Mike's trying to find a place for himself in Los Angeles after moving there from Queens. Just watching Mike feigning savoir-faire, bar hopping with his friends and failing spectacularly with women, is enough to keep the film buoyantly entertaining and deliver a few cautionary lessons, too. For instance: when trying to leave a friendly message on an answering machine, better not use words like desperate or weird.

Mr. Favreau wrote this screenplay with his real friends in mind. And the cast's camaraderie is appealingly clear. Ron Livingston and Patrick Van Horn play other members of this group, all of them hoping to be actors. ["Well, at least it's Disney, right?" says Charles, another pal, who is played by Alex Desert, when one friend nearly lands a job playing Goofy at Disneyland.] Together, they help Mike get shot down by the kinds of women who will sneer at the car he drives or catch him lying about his brilliant career.

In one success story brightly typical of *Swingers,* Mike tries impressing one pickup with the untrue claim that he has an agent. Then she points out that she remembers him from Starbucks. Asking for a job application. Maybe two weeks ago.

PULP FICTION

Roger Ebert
Chicago Sun-Times
June 10, 2001

Dialogue drives Quentin Tarantino's *Pulp Fiction,* dialogue of such high quality it deserves comparison with other masters of spare, hard-boiled prose, from Raymond Chandler to Elmore Leonard. Like them, QT finds a way to make the words humorous without ever seeming to ask for a laugh. Like them, he combines utilitarian prose with flights of rough poetry and wicked fancy.

Howard Hawks once gave his definition of a good movie: "Three good scenes. No bad scenes." Few movies in recent years have had more good scenes than *Pulp Fiction.* Some are almost musical comedy, as when Vincent and Mia dance at Jackrabbit Slim's. Some are stunning in their suddenness, as when Butch returns to his apartment and surprises Vincent. Some are all verbal style, as in Marsellus Wallace's dialogue with Butch.

I saw *Pulp Fiction* for the first time at the Cannes Film Festival in 1994; it went on to win the Palme d'Or, and to dominate the national conversation about film for at least the next 12 months. It is the most influential film of the decade; its circular timeline can be sensed in films as different as *The Usual Suspects, Zero Effect* and *Memento,* not that they copied it, but that they were aware of the pleasures of toying with chronology.

But it isn't the structure that makes *Pulp Fiction* a great film. Its greatness comes from its marriage of vividly original characters with a series of vivid and half-fanciful events and from the dialogue. The dialogue is the foundation of everything else.

MULHOLLAND DRIVE

Manohla Dargis
LA Weekly
October 17, 2001

A dream of the movies as well as a nightmare, David Lynch's newest film is a phantasmagoria of hot bottle blondes, cold-blooded monsters and all the things that go boo in your head. The time is the present, or maybe three weeks ago, or maybe tomorrow. The place is Los Angeles where Sunset Boulevard meets Nightmare Alley, which means that the place is also Hollywood—industry, ideal, crushing dead end.

Here, point of view is everything, including the moral of the story. Lured to L.A. after winning a dance contest, Betty [Naomi Watts] steps into its bleached light as if she were walking onto a sound stage. Dressed in Mary Janes, capris and a 1950s coral sweater studded with rhinestones, she breaks open a smile so wide it's a surprise when she doesn't start singing Rodgers and Hammerstein. Soon afterward, invited to stay at her traveling aunt's empty apartment, she discovers that a brunette with no clothes and no memory [Laura Elena Harring] has already moved into its sprawling, sepulchral rooms. The mystery woman calls herself Rita, having lifted the name off a poster for *Gilda*, and is the survivor of a crackup up on Mulholland, where the movie starts.

While *Mulholland Drive* contains an indictment against the business of movies, it would be too limiting to call the film just another screed against Hollywood. It isn't the dream factory per se that feeds Lynch's rancor; it's the way the factory turns dreams into sausages, people into meat.

CRASH

Lisa Schwarzbaum
Entertainment Weekly
May 4, 2005

The stunning, must-see drama *Crash* is proof that words have not lost the ability to shock in our anesthetized society. I can't remember the last time I have felt so galvanized, disturbed, and moved by full sentences, unadorned by gratuitous profanity, flying out of the mouths of screen characters as ordinary as you or me or the guy idling at the next traffic light on an average day in Los Angeles at Christmastime. *Crash* is about the collision of cars, the machinery on which L.A. is built. But it's also about the collision of races, cultures, and classes—another kind of L.A. experience. White folks, black folks, Hispanics, and Asians—nobody gets by in this amazingly tough, at times unexpectedly funny, and always humane movie without getting dented. An assured directorial debut by *Million Dollar Baby* screenwriter Paul Haggis, who also produced, conceived the story, and wrote the script with Bobby Moresco, *Crash* suggests, convincingly, that violent contact—in word or on wheels—is the only way left to reach out and touch somebody.

Role for role, the acting is superb, and the cinematography is strong, with a stylistic emphasis on blur and confusion interrupted by knife-carved incidents of prejudice and consequence [aurally stitched by Mark Isham's anxious electronic score]. As Haggis' taut vignettes reveal *Crash*'s bigger traffic pattern and the words rain down, there's little to do but grip tight and prepare for major impact.

⫸ AFTER DARK ⫷

Written by **JESSE KATZ** | **THREE MONTHS AFTER** I moved to MacArthur Park, the feverish immigrant district that encompasses the frayed 32-acre oasis of the same name, a white 2011 GMC Sierra came barreling through the neighborhood. The truck was on Wilshire, L.A.'s grand sea-to-skyline boulevard, a street that east of Koreatown and west of downtown bisects the parkland itself. It was 1:20 a.m., a cool, dry October night.

The tires started skidding just below my 13th-story windows, where Wilshire first meets the perimeter of shaggy fan palms and spiky dragon trees. The truck leapt the curb, flattening two parking meters as it fishtailed, then crumpled into the concrete Art Deco balustrade that, in the 1930s, announced the boulevard as our Champs-Élysées. Oil and blood spilled onto the sidewalk. So did flesh, a grisly mash of tissue and muscle, even a severed foot. It would take hours for rescue crews to saw through the wreckage and comb the debris. The driver was arrested. Two passengers were pronounced dead at the scene.

I shudder at it now—the stuff, truly, of nightmares—yet as ghastly as the crash proved to be, I was almost more horrified to learn that I'd slept through it. My first inkling was the impromptu memorial that sprouted the next day, a spread of sunflowers and daffodils, votive candles and metallic balloons. At the center, affixed to the buckled wall with packing tape, was a collection of photos preserved in plastic sleeves. A wedding party. Raised champagne glasses. Toddlers with hair in bows. Lives had been irrevocably shattered right under my nose—the tragedy aided by the very landscape that had drawn me to this corner of the city—and I had been oblivious: a bad neighbor, a somnolent reporter.

MacArthur Park has contained a park since the 1880s, not long after the Southern Pacific Railroad's completion helped transform Los Angeles from a dusty pueblo into a speculator's jamboree. Until then, the alkaline sumphole between 6th and 7th streets had been a foul eyesore; during droughts, the swamp became so crusty it was known as L.A.'s Dead Sea. To turn this neglected hinterland into an open-air resort, the city piped in millions of gallons of fresh water, manufacturing a lake deep enough for boating and fishing and logrolling contests—a "dimple on the face of Nature," as the poet and philanthropist Eliza Otis put it. The lake even hosted the stagecraft of a shackled Harry Houdini, who took the plunge as a crowd of thousands gasped and squirmed.

The park soon bloomed into a lush and rarefied sanctuary, insulated from the tumult of the turn-of-the-century boomtown. There were elegant hotels and smart boutiques and ritzy tearooms on all sides. Mrs. Otis lived at the western edge with the imperious General Harrison Gray Otis, founder of the *Los Angeles Times*, the newspaper that would draw me to L.A. in the 1980s. They called their mansion The Bivouac. Wilshire at the time dead-ended right there, halted by the lake, forcing eastbound traffic north or south. In 1920, after the publisher's death, business leaders commissioned a life-size bronze statue of him, in double-breasted military garb and walrus mustache, and installed it atop a granite boulder at the southeast corner—where it still stands, just steps from the fatal wipeout haunting me now.

"Dangerous Road Is Guarded by Monument," read a headline that year in *Popular Mechanics*, which described the statue as both a tribute and a preventive measure. "A Los Angeles boulevard comes to an end at the edge of a high embankment over a park lake," the magazine explained, adding that "incautious motorists have gone over several times, but with fortunate results."

In an aspiring metropolis of 4,000 square miles—a grid whose defining language is movement—a great boulevard cannot be allowed, of course, to come to a premature end. The campaign to extend Wilshire, to join east and west, to connect the city's historic and political center to the commercial orbit of the Miracle Mile, Beverly Hills, Westwood, and ultimately Santa Monica, thus became something of a civic obsession. In 1922, the *Times* called Wilshire's build-out "the biggest thing yet proposed for the advancement of Los Angeles."

For the next dozen years, L.A. wrestled with the aesthetic and mechanical conundrums of getting Wilshire across or around the lake. The potential fixes, rendered in sketches to aid public debate, ranged from the elegant [bridges, tunnels] to the snide [pontoons, dirigibles]. In the end, city hall embraced the most Angeleno of routes: not over or under but *through* the water, a dirt causeway that would split the park and shrink the lake. It is tempting to conclude that the automobile won that battle—a four-lane thoroughfare cleaving one of L.A.'s oldest green spaces—yet the longer I live here, the greater my doubts about the final score.

To limit costs and preserve as much of the natural landscape as possible, engineers chose to alter Wilshire's trajectory. Rather than a straight shot, the boulevard would bend a few degrees as it traversed the park, a gentle curl to the north that conformed to the lake's reconfigured lip. If Wilshire had been considered a danger before, when it came to an abrupt stop, its arced continuation would create an entirely new kind of obstacle—one magnified by the tide of cars it has been asked to accommodate ever since.

Snipping a garland of roses on December 8, 1934, the mayor called the undertaking the "definition of the spirit of Los Angeles progress." Eighty-plus years later, it would be my dead-man's curve.

They awake me now, the accidents, the knowledge lurking in the recesses of my sleep. Six years of screeches, thuds, hisses, crunches, bursts of glass, whooshes of flame: My brain is conditioned and my ear is attuned. After that first wipeout, I began keeping a tally, my own morbid exercise in neighborhood vigilance. The inevitability of it all made me think of a short story I'd read in high school, "The Holiday Celebrators," in which a gang of wise guys wager on the highway death toll one Labor Day weekend.

I counted two crashes in 2011, two in 2012, one in 2013, two in 2014, three in 2015, and two in 2016. These were just the ones I was home for. I saw a Mercedes-Benz land on its side and a Porsche burst into flames and a Lexus grind ass-end into the concrete. Once, while the police were out on Wilshire sizing up a Mitsubishi Montero that had flipped onto its roof, I watched a Chrysler Sebring slam into the curb and skid nearly up to the squad car—the rare twofer.

Most of these wrecks have occurred between midnight and 4 a.m., as the soju parlors and karaoke lounges a mile or two to the west empty out, and it seems reasonable to assume that some combination of alcohol and exhaustion and darkness conspires to make the bend in Wilshire more like a hairpin. The boulevard till that point is a corridor of faded apartments and modernist offices, a slot canyon that abruptly spills into the gloom of the park. The lake, as viscous as tar, looms ahead; beyond that, skyscrapers rise like beaded curtains. Rather than veering left, the hapless driver continues straight, adrift in the sudden emptiness—until he's on the sidewalk and glissading toward the water. [The protective benefits of General Otis have proved illusory; in 2009, before I moved to MacArthur Park, a young woman died when she plowed her Scion head-first into the statue.]

The lucky ones tend to bail as soon as they come to a stop, disappearing on foot into the shadows of the park. Those too disoriented or injured to run are probably just as stunned to discover that their first responders have emerged from those same shadows. A hundred years after its swankest days, 50 years after Jimmy Webb [with help from Richard Harris and Waylon Jennings and Donna Summer] immortalized it in trippy verse, and 25 years after its gang wars enmeshed the LAPD in what became the Rampart Scandal, MacArthur Park is a modern-day frontier town, a crossroads for the newly arrived and the chronically unwell. The urban jungle now envelops the village green. By day the park is a burbling commons, full of soccer matches and soup kitchens, drum circles and gambling rings, ground zero for Central American evangelists bellowing into bullhorns and Hollywood film crews prowling for noir. After dark it reverts to a squatter's camp, a tagger's canvas,

MACARTHUR PARK IS A MODERN-DAY FRONTIER TOWN, A CROSSROADS FOR THE NEWLY ARRIVED.

a tweaker's playground, which is to say that no matter the hour of the crash someone will be on hand to sound the alarm—even if the rescuers might be as infirm as those needing rescue.

If I manage to fall back asleep, I will sometimes wake in the morning under a hazy spell, wondering if what I witnessed really occurred. I'll wander down and size up the skid marks, pinpointing the exact juncture at which tires breached curb. I'll kick my shoes over the shards of glass, the shreds of rubber, and try to make sense of my adopted neighborhood, its forgotten history, its perpetual thrum.

MacArthur Park was the distraction I thought I needed when my son left for college, the sort of place for a single-dad empty-nester to reboot after two decades in the ethnic burbs. As someone who often writes about L.A.'s margins, I expected the hurly-burly; I didn't expect a street corner to invade my subconscious. The crashes, each a shockingly public event, have become my private ritual.

I tell myself I should probably say something—surely I have an obligation to do more than gawk—and yet I always hesitate, waiting for a sign that what I experience is not invisible to the rest of the city, that somebody else knows or cares. But I already have my answer. You don't notice it at first because it's not there: a 15-foot-long stretch of waist-high concrete that should be wrapping behind General Otis, a segment of the ornamental balustrade that's supposed to cordon off the park from Wilshire. Like the missing teeth of someone too poor or afflicted to see a dentist, the gap expands year by year, each mishap removing a new chunk. L.A. has just learned to live with it.

In the first sentence of his Gen X novel, *Less Than Zero*, Bret Easton Ellis famously wrote: "People are afraid to merge on freeways in Los Angeles." Driving was just another iteration of our estrangement, of lives too alienated and self-involved to care much about anything. In *Crash*, the Oscar-winning morality play, Paul Haggis went further, portraying us as car-cocooned tribes starving for the human contact of a real city: "I think we miss that touch so much that we crash into each other just so we can feel something."

At my corner of Wilshire, the story isn't so much man vs. man or even man vs. machine as man vs. city. The folks missing the turn are neither avoiding their fellow drivers nor colliding with them: They are smacking solo right into the built universe, tripped up by architectural decisions made at a time, long ago, when the city was dismantling its streetcar system and exalting car ownership as the new religion of personal freedom. L.A. rarely pauses to look in the rearview mirror. More than most cities, we hurtle into the future, often without realizing where we've been.

Six times a day, roughly every hour, a cherry-red Starline Tours double-decker bus leaves Hollywood's El Capitan Theatre for the sights of the civic center. The route follows Wilshire for a stretch, and as the bus approaches my apartment, a prerecorded narrator—in a proper British accent, oddly—salutes the neighborhood's place in the pop canon: "We are now entering MacArthur Park...where someone left a cake out in the rain."

The bus usually keeps going—MacArthur Park is not on the official itinerary—but occasionally the driver pulls to the curb to give folks on the open-air deck a steadier photo-op. No picture says L.A. better than the view of downtown from across the lake, a pleasure garden repurposed by refugees sandwiched against a fortress of glass and steel. Where the bus idles for that minute or two is the exact spot—really, you couldn't have aligned it better if you tried—where every car has gone careering off Wilshire. Lately, a homeless encampment has sprung up there, too, a tumble of soiled blankets and flattened cardboard right behind the wall's missing link.

> **WHATEVER IT MEANS TO ANYONE ELSE, ITS SECRET HISTORY REMAINS MINE.**

Nobody, on the bus or in the bushes, would have any reason to know the name David Lee. I do only because he was the driver who, as I slept that October night, decided to gun his truck 85 mph down Wilshire, a 35 mph zone punctuated by stoplights. It is hard to imagine how that could have happened, both the psychology and the physics of it. He was 27 then, an unemployed mortgage processor on his way home to Orange County from a mediocre sports bar a few miles up the street from me. Riding with him were three friends. The two not wearing seat belts were the ones who didn't make it.

I'd always figured the guy must have gone to prison, which I've come to learn he did, though he was required to serve only half his five-year sentence for gross vehicular manslaughter, so he's been out a few years already. As I flipped through the court file recently, one calamitous fact jumped off the page: The dead included Lee's best friend, someone who'd named him godfather to his two little girls. Long before the accident, Lee had vowed to support the children if they were ever left fatherless, and at his sentencing, after he accepted responsibility and expressed remorse, Lee pleaded for leniency, to begin fulfilling that promise as soon as possible. "I can't replace him,"

Lee told the judge, "but I can...fill in his shoes."

Those girls were just one and two years old at the time, too young to understand what had happened. But at some point—assuming Lee follows through, which I want to believe he has—they will come to an awful realization that the man doing right for them is also the man who killed their dad. I can't look at the corner now without that burning in my head.

Whatever this fragment of L.A. geography means to anyone else, to the tourists and the vagabonds, the wide-eyed and the dazed, its secret history remains mine. The bus always moves on. The hobos come and go. But one of these nights, sooner or later, I will be jolted awake.

JESSE KATZ spent 15 years with the *Los Angeles Times* and nine years with *Los Angeles* magazine. Winner of the James Beard Foundation's M.F.K. Fisher Distinguished Writing Award, he is also the author of a memoir, *The Opposite Field*.

⟫ SPRAWL ⟪

Written by **ANN FRIEDMAN** | **LOS ANGELES IS** sometimes referred to as "19 suburbs in search of a metropolis" or "72 suburbs in search of a city," depending on which ad-riddled online compendium of famous quotes you're referencing. The quote is attributed, variously, to Dorothy Parker and Aldous Huxley and H. L. Mencken and Alexander Woollcott, but it doesn't really matter who first committed it to paper. Like nearly everything said about Los Angeles by visiting New York writers, the observation is one that usually only rings true to total outsiders.

To sprawl, in the original Old English, meant to writhe or to lie thrashing about. In other words, sprawl is dynamic. It is a moving, changing thing. This city is indeed an ungainly sprawl of neighborhoods and mini-cities and glorified suburbs and planned communities—anyone in a rented Mustang or sitting on the top of a Gray Line bus can see that. But what these visitors and newcomers usually miss is that L.A.'s disparate parts are not in search of anything; they are thrashing in dozens of different directions.

Every big city is a loose coalition of distinct neighborhoods, but the sheer spread of L.A. makes it particularly easy to feel untethered from the whole. Here, the neighborhoods' very association is looser than in other places. And those of us who have come to love this place understand this as a cultural advantage—or, at the very least, a charming quirk. It's up to individuals to seek the city, and that search creates their personal center.

Finding the center of Los Angeles is a process that is not always appealing or immediately apparent—even to those of us who have been through it ourselves. And this fact can make it difficult to defend Los Angeles to skeptics or to persuade new transplants to embrace its quirks. When I convinced my boyfriend to move from London to Los Angeles a few years ago, he struggled to apply his European notions of urban wayfinding to his new California landscape. We lived just north of downtown, which initially provided some comfort that he was not exchanging true city life for an endless expanse of freeway-linked suburbs. But he quickly realized that here, "downtown" is not synonymous with "city center." Unlike cities that are neatly demarcated by zones or arrondissements or postcodes that clearly mark the distance from a central point, Los Angeles refuses to agree on its core. The center is wherever you decide it is.

But it was difficult for me to articulate this to him. It had never occurred to me that a lack of geographic center was one of Los Angeles' shortcomings as a city. Sure, we'd all like more comprehensive public transit and fewer guys with shirts unbuttoned to their navels and a better source of water than the Colorado River, 242 miles away. But a common, agreed-upon center? It was so far down my urban wish list that it hadn't even registered. For me, like most Angelenos, the center is a subjective concept. In my case, it's near the meeting of Echo Park Avenue and Sunset Boulevard—a junction where crucial elements such as the House of Spirits liquor store, a solid Walgreens, a fish-taco spot, several good bus lines, and a vegan restaurant come together.

My personal center is marked not just by the landmarks on the ground, but by the sound of helicopters circling above. It lies in a hilly patch of land between the 101 and 110 and 5 freeways, which makes it prime flyover territory for medical airlifts and traffic reports and aerial police chases. After I struggled to defend L.A.'s lack of agreed-upon center, this hyperlocal helicopter noise made me start to wonder if I might be able to better observe the city's loose union of neighborhoods and suburbs from the air. Maybe I was wrong: Perhaps Los Angeles really does have a unified, definable center—geographical or otherwise—and I was simply grounded, unable to see it. Maybe the city's natural boundaries, like mountains and freeways, are a centralizing force. At the very least, from above, I might be able to better figure out what unites us. Palm trees and bougainvillea? A view of the hills? Hot concrete?

A quick Google search leads me to Celebrity Helicopters, which is at the center of its own very L.A. Venn diagram: It's a Compton-based aerial sightseeing company that caters to both tourists and Hollywood ["tours seen on *The Bachelor*!"] while doubling as a flight training school for kids from the neighborhood. I convince owner

Robin Petgrave to let me tag along on one of his sightseeing flights. Robin was a transplant himself. Born in Jamaica and raised in Boston, he had a tough childhood in and out of foster care. Eventually, he found sports and went to college on a track scholarship. He moved to Los Angeles after graduation because he wanted to make it as an actor. But he'd always wanted to learn to fly, and he enrolled in a small flight school. From there he built his own helicopter company. His personal successes led him to create Tomorrow's Aeronautical Museum, where he teaches kids about aviation history and plants the seed that they, too, can become pilots. It's a classic L.A. story of coming here to chase a Hollywood dream and falling in love with the city instead. [What, you've never heard that one? Trust me, it's more common than you think.]

On this hazy, sunny fall day, a visitor named Luisa has booked a tour of L.A.'s celebrity homes and natural vistas. After a short wait in the office—kids who are enrolled in a tutoring program are running around, so it feels very much like a community center—Robin walks us out to the helicopter. Luisa sits in front with Robin. I sit in the back seat with a trainee pilot named Lucky, who explains to me that piloting a helicopter is much more difficult than flying a plane. For the first and only time, I feel a twinge of nervousness.

But we take off, and the feeling dissipates as I'm distracted by the city unfolding beneath me. It quickly becomes apparent that, even from the air, everyone's center of Los Angeles is different. Robin begins pointing out landmarks: "This is where Ice Cube and Kendrick Lamar are from. Those are the tennis courts where Venus and Serena Williams practiced. This is Watts, where the model Tyrese grew up." We climb to 600 feet and veer north. "Those are the Jordan Downs Projects, where they filmed *Training Day* and *Menace II Society*." I'm guessing that Robin's center of L.A. is somewhere between Compton and black Hollywood. He also points out our common landmarks [the freeways, the mountains]. Looking down on it from the air, Robin is in his element.

To me, though, so far being up this high just feels like being on a plane landing at LAX: miles of concrete in all directions. No sight of my personal center. No grand theories on what holds this city together. The helicopter approaches downtown, where the buildings look like they could scrape our thin metal underbelly. For the first

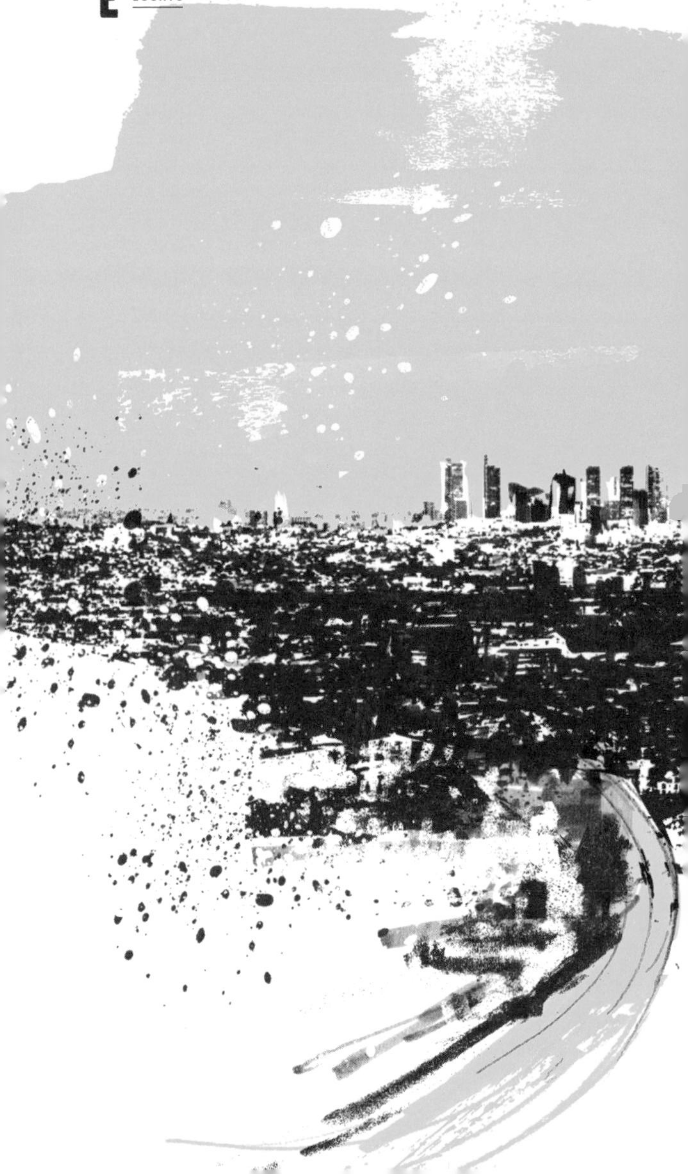

time since takeoff, I feel light-headed. Robin instructs us to point our phone cameras out the left side window and angle them downward, then proceeds to take a sharp circle around the US Bank Tower. When I watch the video later, I hear myself giggling coyly as if the city itself is flirting with me. This is where my romantic notions of thrashing sprawl threaten to break down. I feel closest to my city here, hovering above its conventionally defined city center. This isn't how it was supposed to go.

The architectural historian Reyner Banham, who was quite turned on by L.A.'s defiance of traditional urbanism, nevertheless sought to impose some order on our centerless city. He divided Los Angeles into four "ecologies": the beaches of Surfurbia, the mansions of the Foothills, the valley-floor Plains of Id, and the freeways of Autopia. He relegated downtown, the stereotypical city center, to a sidenote. Each skyscraper and landmark of downtown L.A., he wrote, "stands as an unintegrated fragment in a downtown scene that began to disintegrate long ago—out of sheer irrelevance, as far as one can see."

From the ground—even if you appreciate the easy beauty of Broadway's strip of old movie theaters or feel charmed by Frank Gehry's concert hall or hollowed out by the rows of tents on Skid Row—it's easy to agree with Banham. But from the air, this is the first part of the tour that's felt distinct, like we're really getting somewhere. As we spin among the buildings, a sense of scale finally emerges. Up here, downtown is relevant.

Just as quickly, we leave it behind. We fly over my personal center, near Dodger Stadium, and for once I'm one of those thwapping noises that usually haunt me from above. I search for my center below. But even though I know all of the landmarks, we pass so quickly that I can't lay eyes on the Walgreens or the liquor store or my house. I've only gotten context clues.

But I barely have time to think about it because we're on to Griffith Park, where the dusty hills and observatory rise into our frame of reference just as the downtown buildings did. And I realize that downtown is not the center of L.A., it's just that the height of the helicopter creates its own center: It prioritizes the vertical, and so the hills of Griffith are just as breathtaking as the skyscrapers downtown.

As he maneuvers the helicopter through the hills, offering our first glimpse of the San Fernando Valley beyond, Robin continues to remind us of his own center. He points out places of interest below: "That's Universal Studios, where they shot *Blazing Saddles*. And these are the Hollywood Hills—that's Halle Berry's house. That's Lionel Richie's house. That used to be Eddie Murphy's house." Robin and Lucky can't believe it when they spot the helicopter from *AirWolf*— the 1980s TV series about a tricked-out military helicopter's espionage missions—on display on the meticulously manicured grounds of a mansion. Robin triple-checks to make sure Lucky has gotten some good photos.

An hour later—long after we've flown the length of Malibu and Santa Monica at 135 mph over the blue-green water—they'll still be talking about seeing "the real AirWolf." And I'll still be thinking about how, even though I saw Halle Berry's house, I couldn't place my personal center from the air. It's as if, from high above, I lost a bit of my ownership of the city. Back on the ground, after I've skirted the edges of rush hour on unfamiliar side streets and found my way home, I'm recentered. And only then do I really relate to those skeptical outsiders and newcomers, and understand how tough it can be to chart this place for yourself—even though the payoff is incredible.

When non-locals remark on L.A.'s lack of center, it always seems that they are expressing unease at the deeper realization that no one is in charge here. L.A. was mostly shaped in haphazard reaction to population growth and human behavior and the whims of a few rich folks—not by urban planning vision or military strategy. It's not just "new" in the sense that its oldest landmarks are less than a century old. It's new because its geography is constantly being replotted and its sprawl is dynamic. It's new because you can't be sure what it will look like in three days, let alone 30 years. And on days that take you high up and far away from your routine, miles from the thrashing neighborhood you've chosen to tame for yourself, you can't even be certain that your own center will hold. The suburbs are not in search of a city. You are the one who must do the searching.

ANN FRIEDMAN *has written for the* Los Angeles Times, The Gentlewoman *and* New Republic, *among others, as well as for* NYMag.com. *Her podcast and Friday email newsletter are highly recommended.*

⫸ PAGE ONE ⫷

From the **LOS ANGELES TIMES**

On April 29, 1992, a trial jury acquitted four white Los Angeles police officers charged with the use of excessive force in the beating of an unarmed black man, Rodney Glen King, III. The vicious encounter was captured on a home video by a nearby resident, showing the officers' 56 baton swings and six kicks on King. More than a year after the incident, the acquittal lit a fuse to racial tensions in L.A., intensifying into widespread looting, arson and general mayhem, that peaked in the two days following the trial. Fifty-five people were killed and more than 11,000 arrested in scenes that took on the atmosphere of a war zone. The Los Angeles Times *newspaper coverage of the riots garnered a Pulitzer Prize for "Spot News Reporting," which included 33 staff writers sharing bylines on ten stories from the second day of unrest. The excerpts below are taken directly from the reportage and storytelling on May 1, 1992. The articles here appear exactly as they did on that day's front page, except for the final entry, which appeared on page 3.*

LOOTING AND FIRES RAVAGE L.A.

25 DEAD, 572 INJURED, 1,000 BLAZES REPORTED

UNREST: Troops begin deployment and a dusk-to-dawn curfew is clamped into place in the second day of violence

BY GREG BRAXTON AND JIM NEWTON
Times Staff Writers

Thousands of looters ransacked stores and set fires Thursday in a chaotic rampage through the Los Angeles area as National Guard troops moved into the streets and a dusk-to-dawn curfew was clamped into force in numerous cities.

With the violence showing no signs of abating, Gov. Pete Wilson and Mayor Tom Bradley announced just before midnight that they have requested additional National Guard troops for a total of 6,000 in Los Angeles County. They said they have also asked federal authorities to place U.S. military forces on "standby alert" should greater strength become necessary.

"We are determined," Wilson said, "that this city is not going to suffer the kind of terrorizing that some people seem bent on inflicting upon it."

Triggered by Wednesday's not guilty verdicts of four Los Angeles police officers charged with beating black motorist Rodney G. King, the second day of mushrooming violence pushed the death toll to 25, including eight people shot by police. Another 572 injuries were reported, 100 of them critical.

In a period of little more than 24 hours, about 1,000 structural fires were reported in Los Angeles County. It seemed as though, with each passing moment, fresh flames rose from new locations, sending ripples of fear through neighborhoods close to and miles away from the mayhem. Preliminary damage figures were being put at $200 million. Authorities have made more than 700 arrests.

As dusk approached, Police Commission President Stanley K. Sheinbaum said even the National Guard and the California Highway Patrol will not be enough to quiet the spreading unrest.

"The problem is widening, intensifying," Sheinbaum said. "You have a whole social upheaval."

Unlike the Watts riots of 1965, the violence this time has not been confined to an isolated area. Looters pilfered merchandise from mini-malls and swap meets through a combat zone that stretched from near downtown, into South Los Angeles, through the heart of Hollywood and toward the Westside.

In incidents reminiscent of what happened in Los Angeles on Wednesday night, some whites in Long Beach were attacked by angry black demonstrators, who reportedly killed one man and injured at least 15 people, according to police and hospital officials.

A mob of about 15 rioters attacked two men on a motorcycle

as they drove near Lemon Avenue and 20th Street, killing one of the men when he was shot in the back.

*Please see RIOT, A*10

+++

SOUTH L.A. BURNS AND GRIEVES

Life has been hard in the neglected area for years. But now, as self-inflicted wounds mount, residents fear for the future.

BY JONATHAN PETERSON AND HÉCTOR TOBAR

Times Staff Writers

In a smoky parking lot in South Los Angeles, Ruby Galude, 55, stared in disbelief at the wreckage of her local grocery store. "I'm a diabetic. This is where I get all my juices and foods," she said, peering at shards of glass and soaked debris. "What am I going to do now?"

A few miles away, Paul C. Hudson arrived at his family-run savings and loan, a community fixture since 1947 in a neighborhood that has a grave shortage of banks. On Wednesday night it burned down. "Just the exterior wall was left standing," he said.

Anthony Wright and his wife, Jaye, meanwhile, sat in lawn chairs, as radio news blared from their pickup truck. Just a few blocks away, hundreds of people were on a looting rampage on Vermont Avenue.

Hard times fuel the fury, said Jaye Wright, a teacher's aide. "It's not a recession for minority communities. It's a depression."

Long before this week's spasm of destruction, daily life in part of South Los Angeles was grueling in ways much different from elsewhere in the city. In ordinary, mundane ways—from a shortage of grocery stores and credit at normal interest rates to a scarcity of jobs and the more publicized ills of crime and drugs—it was often hard to get through a typical day.

Now, the rising toll in human life, torched businesses and destroyed property are adding insult to an already dangerous, frustrating existence.

On Thursday, some residents spoke in determined voices about getting on with the job of rebuilding their community. There were brave pronouncements of commitment to the future, promises that shellshocked South Los Angeles would pick itself up and, with the aid of new investment, move forward after the rioting subsides.

"We have an obligation to reopen," said Hudson, president of Broadway Federal Savings & Loan, whose green, two-story headquarters on 45th Street survived the Watts riots but not the current mayhem.

However, there were other voic-

Please see FEAR, A24

+++

OPPORTUNISTS, CRIMINALS GET BLAME FOR RIOTS

BY VICTOR MERINA AND JOHN MITCHELL
Times Staff Writers

As Los Angeles firefighters and police spent a weary day and night battling arson blazes and looters, stunned residents and business owners grappled with the question of who is torching and pillaging their communities. The answer seemed to be both criminals and opportunists.

The rampage, which began Wednesday within hours of the verdicts in the Rodney G. King beating case, continued Thursday with scenes reminiscent of a war zone—smoke billowing from dozens of fires, looters hustling out of stores with merchandise and gunfire echoing through the streets periodically.

But amid the pall, there also was a carnival atmosphere among some participants and onlookers who raced to stricken neighborhoods to watch, join the looting or record events with video cameras. And there was the bizarre picture of gleeful teenagers and families, as if on a weekend outing, ignoring outnumbered police and loading up on looted goods.

Although young black men constituted many of the rioters and—
*Please see RIOTERS, A*12

+++

LAPD SLOW IN COPING WITH WAVE OF UNREST

*RESPONSE: But the rapidly unfolding violence might
have overwhelmed any police department*

BY DAVID FREED AND TED ROHRLICH

Times Staff Writers

Where were the police?

That was the question that many in Los Angeles, including members of the city's Police Department, were asking Thursday in the aftermath of televised beatings, burning and looting that raged for hours in South Los Angeles before officers made any attempt to stop it.

Even Chief Daryl F. Gates, who insisted beforehand that the LAPD was ready for "any emergency situation," conceded that his officers were overwhelmed by how quickly the crisis developed and were "much too slow" to respond.

"I asked the same question: Where were the police?" Gates told reporters. "We moved in with substantial numbers but not with the numbers needed to handle the situation."

Gates speculated, however, that had LAPD officers not retreated when rioting first flared, they might have incited even greater violence.

But as the chief sought to defend his actions, the crisis demonstrated the grave difficulties encountered by the Police Department in the first hours of the worst urban turmoil in Los Angeles since the 1965 Watts riots.

*Please see RESPONSE, A*11

JURORS RATTLED BY AFTERMATH; DEFEND VERDICTS

BY PAUL LIEBERMAN AND STUART SILVERSTEIN
Times Staff Writers

Some of the jurors fled their homes, fearful for their lives. Others retreated behind locked doors and struggled to comprehend the violent aftermath of their verdicts.

At least two, shaken to the edge of tears, wondered whether they could possibly be responsible for the rioting and fires that were spreading through Los Angeles.

"I've gotten some calls saying that I'll have to live with this for-
Please see JURORS, A17

+++

BEATEN DRIVER A SEARING IMAGE OF MOB CRUELTY

BY LAURIE BECKLUND AND STEPHANIE CHAVEZ
Times Staff Writers

At every watershed through time, it seems a face emerges to transfix a moment in history. In Vietnam, a naked girl fled in napalm. In Tian An Men Square, a single student stared down a line of Chinese tanks. In Los Angeles last year, Rodney G. King lay prone and beaten.

Now, a white gravel truck driver beaten nearly into oblivion in South Los Angeles has become the face on the flip side of the Rodney King coin, the unofficial black-on-white response to the official white-on-black beating.

His name is Reginald Oliver Denny. He is 36. He is alive because four strangers—four black strangers who saw him dragged from his truck and beaten nearly to death—emerged from the crowd to drive his unwieldy 18-wheeler out of pandemonium to safety.

The rescuers were two women and two men, a young nutrition consultant, a laid-off data control worker, an unemployed aerospace worker and a still-unidentified young man in black whose fellow rescuers first feared was a gangbanger coming to finish Denny off.

Please see DRIVER, A14

+++

VIEW OF MODEL MULTIETHNIC CITY VANISHES IN SMOKE

RELATIONS: Disturbances bare a simmering racial anger that community efforts never fully quelled.

BY STEPHEN BRAUN AND ASHLEY DUNN

Times Staff Writers

Like a bandage stripped off an open wound, the civil unrest sweeping through South Los Angeles in the last two days has exposed and intensified the painful strains of racial anger and ethnocentrism that have long simmered among the city's myriad ethnic communities.

The popular notion advanced by Mayor Tom Bradley and other civic leaders in recent years that Los Angeles was transforming itself into a harmonious, multiethnic model city appeared to waft away amid the acrid smoke billowing over the city.

Each new graphic televised image—black, Latino and white looters rampaging through ruined stores, white police officers and National Guard soldiers advancing to retake city streets by force, dazed white and Latino passersby beaten by angry black assailants, frightened Korean merchants guarding their shuttered markets with guns—threatened to reinforce the long-held fears and prejudices gnawing at the city's populace, worried community leaders and race relations experts said Thursday.

The countless scenes of South Los Angeles residents rushing to

help strangers caught in the crossfire were obscured by the onslaught-
Please see RACE, A28

+++

A LONG NIGHT OF ANGER, ANARCHY

RIOTS: Some Good Samaritans brave violent mobs and jittery police to aid the injured.

BY CHARISSE JONES AND DEAN E. MURPHY
Times Staff Writers

Carlos Mejia was one of the lucky ones. He had a large bandage taped to his head and dried blood smudged on his face, but he was leaving the hospital alive.

Mejia was driving near Manchester Boulevard and Western Avenue on his way to pick up his cousin at work when a mob converged on his car Wednesday night.

"Five came from one side, and five came from the other," he said outside the hospital, still dazed hours later. "They asked me if I—
Please see NIGHT, A29

+++

UPSET AND UNGLUED, KING STAYS BEHIND A LOCKED DOOR

BY RICHARD A. SERRANO
Times Staff Writer

Stunned, speechless and shaking, Rodney G. King retreated late in the afternoon to the solitude of his bedroom.

On the television screen, the four Los Angeles police officers accused of beating him had just been found not guilty. They were hugging and smiling in the courtroom. But King, the 26-year-old Altadena motorist whose life took a dramatic turn on a midnight drive in the San Fernando Valley 14 months ago, locked himself inside his bedroom.

The lights were turned off; the television was down low. Through the doorjamb, his occasional screams could be heard. "Why? Why? Why?" he groaned. "Why are they beating me again?"

As night came, and rioters and looters spread mayhem on city streets, King still refused to come out of the bedroom, according to recollections Thursday from relatives, friends and members of King's growing legal entourage.

By 10 p.m., a psychiatrist was called in.

Please see KING, A11

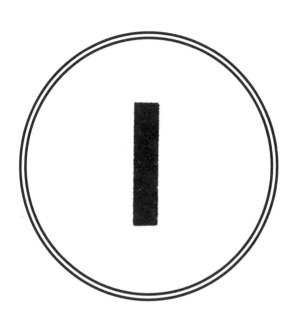

INDEX

⫸ INDEX ⫷

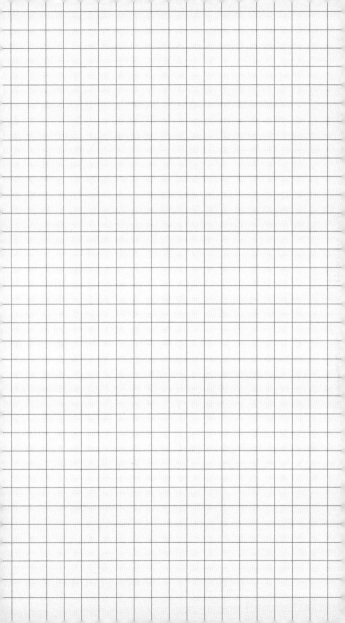

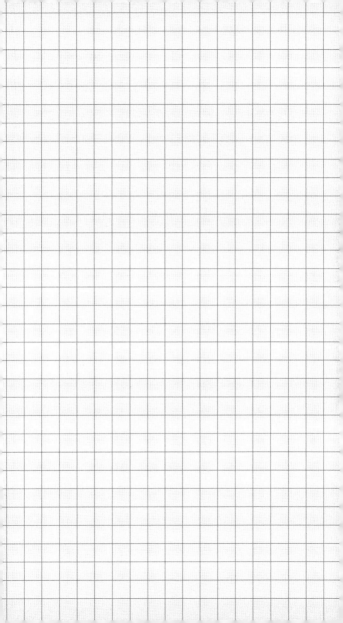